THE BEST Angel STORIES

THE BEST

Angel

STORIES

EDITORS OF

GUIDEPOSTS

Conari Press

This edition first published in 2015 by Conari Press
an imprint of Red Wheel/Weiser, LLC
With offices at:
665 Third Street, Suite 400
San Francisco, CA 94107
www.redwheelweiser.com

Permissions and Acknowledgments can be found on p. 267.

Library of Congress Cataloging-in-Publication Data available upon request.

ISBN: 978-1-57324-677-4

Cover design by Jim Warner
Cover illustration copyright © 2015 Nadia Strelkina licensed by MGL.
  www.mgllicensing.com
Interior design by Müllerhaus
Typesetting by Aptara, Inc.

Printed in the United States of America
MG
10 9 8 7 6 5 4 3 2 1

Contents

Chapter 1
Shielded by Their Wings

Chapter 2
Messengers of Love

Chapter 3
Glimpses of Heaven

Contents

Chapter 4
Mysterious Knowings

Contents

Chapter 5
Touched through Time

Chapter 6
Animal Angels

Contents

Special Section
Children and Angels

Introduction

INNER VOICES, MYSTERIOUS STRANGERS, FEELINGS of inexplicable peace in times of adversity . . . I know stories of just such happenings. As editor-in-chief of Angels on Earth magazine, I've heard hundreds of awesome stories over the years, told to me by readers, family members and friends alike. Th ese true personal expe-riences, of miracles big and small, share a powerful message. Th ey recall my favor-ite Psalm, chapter 91, verse 11 (NIV): "For he will command his angels concerning you to guard you all ways." Th ese stories are proof that God and His angels are at work in our everyday worlds.

Here we have collected more than eighty stories about real people who've had real encounters with real angels. Whether the angels appear as a cloud of butterfl ies, or a strain of heavenly music, or adorned with wings and robes, these messengers bring the reassurance that we are never alone. We are watched over, cared for, and loved.

We've chosen the best angel stories of the year, including classic stories from our own Angels on Earth magazine, as well as our favorite stories from other sources and all-new stories that have never been told anywhere. You'll meet people who have experienced impossible rescues and amazing protection, people who have received messages of love and comfort from beyond, people wh o have died and visited heaven before returning to tell us what they've seen. You'll see how the innocence of a child or the loyalty of a beloved pet can draw angels to your side.

Curl up with this collection and a cup of tea, and catch a glimpse of the otherworldly hidden in our midst. And, as always, if you have an angel story of your own, please share it with me. Send a manuscript with a self-addressed stamped envelope to our editorial offi ce, Angels on Earth, 16 East 34 Street, New York, New York 10016, or via e-mail to submissions@angelsonearth.org.

—Colleen Hughes
Angels on Earth Editor-in-Chief

THE BEST Angel STORIES

CHAPTER 1

Shielded by Their Wings

Our Evening Walk

Donna Griffith

MOM AND I ALWAYS RELIED on one another. I worked at a fast food restaurant, but before and after my shifts she served me the best home-cooked breakfasts and dinners a girl could want. Plus she gave expert foot rubs, which came in handy. But most of all I looked forward to our evening walks.

One evening we walked down the road to the first major intersection. "Look both ways before you cross," Mom said.

"Always the mother hen," I replied. *Always trying to take care of me. Just like I'm always trying to take care of her. Lord, I wish we had someone to take care of both of us.*

There weren't any cars coming, so we stepped into the crosswalk. Halfway across the street I heard screeching wheels. A late-model sedan was barreling right for us. There was no time to run. "Jesus," I mumbled, braced for impact.

That's when I felt them: two strong hands on my upper arms. The car was so close I could make out specks of dirt on the shiny front grille. But the second before a collision happened, I was lifted into the air. I felt a rush of wind as the car passed me. Somehow I had been taken out of harm's way just in time.

The next thing I knew I was sitting on the sidewalk across the street, the cool concrete under my palms. *Mom!* I expected to see her lying injured in the road.

Chris got out, her feet plunging into a high snow drift, and she looked around. *Lord, please send us some help*, she prayed. Then she saw it—a silo and barn roof peeking up from the hills, about a quarter-mile away. "Mom," Chris leaned in the car, "I'll walk down to that barn and see if anyone's there. Keep the kids warm."

The journey was incredibly cold, and by the time Chris pushed open the barn door, her feet were icy. A welcome blast of heat greeted her, along with the mooing of heifers in their stalls. It was a working dairy, clean and well organized, with a shiny window fan circulating the air.

Even better, Chris heard young male voices behind a stall. Maneuvering around fresh manure, she followed the sound and came upon two farmhands in overalls and flannel shirts, kidding and teasing each other. They stopped and smiled when they saw her, and she quickly explained the situation.

"Stay here!" one said, tramping past the cows and out the door. A few moments later, Chris heard a horn honking in front of the barn. There he was, driving a blue pickup truck. "Get in!" he shouted.

Chris hesitated. She didn't know these men. And yet there was something so merry about them that she couldn't feel afraid. She and the other farmhand scrambled into the pickup and bounced down the road. There was the car, her toddlers bundled up and Mom waving. The driver roared across the field, spun in a wide circle and screeched into position in front of it. "Way to go!" his buddy yelled.

Chris gripped the seat. "Do you always drive like this?" she asked, only half-joking.

The driver shrugged. "Well, it ain't our truck."

Within minutes, the men had freed Chris's car, and she opened her purse to reward them. But both backed away. "It was our pleasure, ma'am. Just drive safely."

You mean, not like you? Chris thought to herself, grinning as she pulled away. *What wonderful guys.*

Chris didn't realize just how wonderful until two weeks later when she and her mother decided to make a return visit to her grandmother. Since the snow was almost melted now, the shortcut was safer. Soon the silo and barn roof came into view.

"Let's stop and let the guys know we made it to Grandma's that day," Chris suggested. But when they pulled up in front of the barn where Chris had climbed into the blue truck, she could hardly believe her eyes.

For the barn was vacant, shabby, with paint peeling and door hinges hanging loose. Bewildered, Chris wiped away a heavy film of dirt and cobwebs on the milk house window and peered inside. Where were the heifers? Where were the floors littered with fresh manure? Even the fan was rusty.

"You couldn't have seen any farmhands or cattle there," the woman at the next house told Chris when she went to inquire. "No one's worked that property for years."

Chris got in the car. "Am I crazy, Mom?" she asked.

"No." Her mother was firm. "This is definitely the place."

Then how…?

Suddenly Chris understood, and like the shepherds at that first Christmas, she was filled with awe. Her angels had worn blue jeans instead of white robes. But they had delivered the same timeless message to her and to anyone willing to listen: Fear not. The Savior is here, and He cares about you. Hallelujah!

Rescue in the Rapids

Jennifer Kelly

WE LOUNGED ON INNER TUBES, floating lazily down the river. It was August and some co-workers had invited me along on a weekend getaway, tubing Wisconsin's Apple River. The river was a hugely popular tubing spot. Already, only a few minutes after we'd entered the water, other tubers were joining our flotilla. At least twenty of us drifted in the gentle current, our tubes lashed together with thick twine. We talked, ate and drank, and watched the wooded banks glide by.

It was the first time I'd relaxed in months. All of a sudden everything had changed in my life. I'd moved to a new town in Wisconsin, gotten a new job and broken up with a guy I'd been dating for seven years. When people I worked with asked if I wanted to go tubing, I said yes. I wasn't much of an outdoors person, but I'd been so lonely lately and this was my chance to make some new friends. I hoped I could handle the rapids. So far all had gone well. We'd arrived Friday afternoon—and we had enough time to try a test run down the river. The weekend crowds were just trickling in so the river was calm and quiet. Even the rapids I'd worried about had turned out to be fun. They were shallow and not too fast. The tubes swooped and bounced over rocks and waves. As long as you held on you were fine.

Today was Saturday and it was like a different river. A traffic jam of tubes clogged the water. Total strangers bumped into us, and before we knew it they were tied onto our tubes like they'd known us forever. I couldn't help noticing one handsome guy who tied onto my tube near the back of the flotilla. He looked just about my age, mid-twenties, with dark, close-cut hair and a tank top that showed off tan, muscled arms. I tried a few times to talk to him but he didn't seem interested in conversation. He was never rude. Just seemed to want to be by himself. I had others to talk to.

The ride down the river lasted four hours. The rapids came just before the end. Soon, in the distance, we heard the loud rush of swirling water. "Rapids up ahead!" someone called out. "Bathroom break."

We paddled the flotilla to a bank lined with portable toilets. I was one of the last to go, and when I came back I saw someone had taken my tube. I didn't mind. We didn't have far to go. I jumped onto the cooler tube, a smaller inner tube they give you at the rental shop for carrying an ice chest. Someone had put the ice chest on their own tube so the cooler tube was free. I'm small so I fit fine. I looked for the handsome guy. He was still in his tube not far away.

We pushed back out into the river. I noticed that with so many tubes tied together we were floating much faster than we had the day before. I looked at my little cooler tube. My legs and arms hung way outside. All it would take was one good bounce on those rapids and I'd be in the water.

Small waves formed atop the current. The riverbank whizzed past then rose into steep cliffs. I saw white water in the distance and felt the flotilla drift to one side, following the flow of the river. We swung around until my little tube was closest to the bank. All of a sudden I saw something large and white speeding toward me. It was some kind of plastic culvert embedded in the embankment. I gripped my tube as it struck the culvert, bending like a bicycle tire rammed into a curb. Before I knew it I was hurled into the air and landed face first in the water.

The flotilla shot down the rapids. I felt a sharp pain in my left bicep and realized somehow the twine lashing my tube to the other tubes had gotten wrapped around my arm. I was dragged through the water, slamming against rocks, unable to get my head up. The twine kept me trapped against the tube. I was in shock. I knew my body was taking a terrible beating but I couldn't feel a thing.

I remembered the day before it had taken about ten minutes to get through the rapids. No way could I hold my breath that long. I heaved as hard as I could and barely got my head up to take a gulp of air. Then I was slammed down again. No one, I figured, had seen me go under. They'd be looking down river. *Don't panic, Jennifer.* If I thrashed around I'd just use up more oxygen. *It doesn't matter,* I thought. I had no more strength to lift my head. I was about to suffocate. I was going to die.

Suddenly in my mind's eye—or did I open my eyes?—I saw surrounding me a circle of faces. The faces were calm, encouraging. They didn't say anything and I didn't recognize any of them. But I knew they were real. I relaxed. I feared nothing.

The next moment I felt a powerful grip on my right arm and I was hauled out of the water. The dark-haired man I'd seen earlier was standing beside me, his hand clamped to my arm. He'd jumped off his tube and somehow planted his feet on the rocky bottom. My arm was still tangled in the twine. The flotilla jerked to a halt, tugging me with unbearable force. My head went under the water. Vaguely I heard the man shouting. People began jumping off their tubes, trying to push the flotilla to shore. The man must have realized there was no time. He let go my arm, grabbed the wet twine—it was at least an inch-and-a-half thick—and ripped it apart. The flotilla spun away. The man lifted me from the water and I wrapped my arms around his neck.

"Oh my God! Thank you!" I coughed. He sloshed his way to the riverbank and set me down. "What's your name?" I asked. But before I could say more my new friends were around me with frightened faces. I strained to see the dark-haired man. I thought I glimpsed him walking away. Then he was gone.

I never saw the man again. I searched the shore, asked everyone on the bus back to the camping area and scoured the campground itself. No one had seen him. No one knew who he was. By that point I was feeling every one of those rocks that had bashed into me. I lay in my tent thinking about the man. Not just because he'd saved my life. But because in some strange way that awful moment beneath the water—those calm faces, that strong grip on my arm—reassured me that no matter how lonely I might ever feel, I would never truly be alone. That man was my guardian angel. His strong, silent strength will be with me always.

Snow Rescue

Katherine Ruhlman

SKIING WAS ALL I HAD on my mind. There was nothing I liked more than grabbing my cross-country skis on a sunny winter day and leaving everything else behind. I drove out to the local nature preserve. There was real freedom in being out there alone, just me, the snow, and the sky.

The day was so beautiful, I stayed out way later than I should have. *How can I go back to my day-to-day life when I have all of this?* I thought as I whizzed down a small slope. The sky darkened, and the wind picked up. *Better get home before it really starts snowing.* I was only about a half hour from my car. The flakes were coming down faster and faster as I moved down the trail back to the parking lot. Soon I could barely see ten feet in front of me.

I left the trail and headed in a straight line down the sloping hill. I zoomed along until it got too dense, dark, and snowy to keep going safely at that pace. "Oh, God," I croaked. "It's going to be a whiteout."

Gusts of wind pelted my face with snow. I pulled my coat tightly around me and tied my scarf around my head. I groped behind me trying to find the trail, but all I saw around me was snow, snow, and more snow. Now I didn't know which end was up.

I got down on one knee. *Lord, please help me not to panic.*

I stood up, picked a direction, and tried to make my way back toward the parking lot. I could only hope it was the right way. Time seemed to pass slower as I got more and more worried. *How do you know you're even going in the right direction?* I asked myself. *What if you're going the wrong way?* My glorious afternoon had turned into a real nightmare. I toppled into a snowbank. "Help me, God," I cried. "Don't let me die here!"

I pushed myself back onto my feet. It was hard to even stand against the violent gusts. I pushed on. "Give me strength, God," I said. It was pitch black outside. My body was failing. I wanted to sleep, but that would be deadly. I fell into another snowbank. This time, I didn't have the strength to pull myself up. I struggled helplessly against the dense snow. "Please, God," I begged. "This is as far as I can go."

Suddenly, I heard a crunching sound in the distance. I pulled myself up as far as I could. "Hello!" I called. "Hello! Can you hear me?"

Out of the darkness skied a young man. "Ski over to that tree and make a left," he said, helping me up. "There's a small rangers' shed. You can warm up inside."

I looked to where he was pointing and saw the little shack. He gripped my arm. "When the storm lets up, follow that trail behind the house back to the parking lot. Go! Now!"

With that, he skied off down the mountain. I pushed my way to the shed and let myself in. I sat down and warmed up by the heating vent. I checked myself for frostbite.

Everything seemed okay. I closed my eyes and waited. It was almost midnight by the time the snow slowed to a gentle flurry.

Sure enough, the path was where the young man had told me it would be. I skied past the spot where I'd collapsed and found the imprint in the snow where I'd almost met my end. I could see my tracks still in the snow, too, heading over the shed. But when I looked down the path in the direction the young man had gone, I couldn't see any ski tracks at all. Just fresh fallen snow. *But how…?* I wondered. I had no answer.

I followed the trail and found my car. I started the engine, turned the heat on high, and took off my gear. I laid my head on the steering wheel, still in shock over my miraculous rescue. I knew if that young man hadn't helped me, I wouldn't be sitting there feeling the heat from the car. *Only You could have done this*, I prayed to God. *Thank You.*

To this day, whenever I see a blizzard anywhere I'm reminded to lift my eyes and whisper, "Thank you." I still love leaving it all behind to go skiing. But the one thing I never leave behind is God. And I know He never leaves me either. Not even in the worst of snowstorms.

An Angel in Every Lap

Joan Wester Anderson

THE TRIP STARTED OUT AS hundreds of others did. Lorie Torbeck of Appleton, Wisconsin, helped by her teenage daughter, Eryn, buckled the seven children who attended Lorie's home day care into their seats in her big Chevy Suburban to go to the high school.

"Eryn was a cheerleader, and it was yearbook picture day for the team," Lorie later recalled. "The kids and I had made this quick trip dozens of times."

Now, as they were driving along a narrow stretch of highway, a white panel truck came toward them. Lorie moved onto the shoulder to give the truck ample room to pass. But as she tried to return to the highway, her tires became stuck in a six-inch drop from the concrete to the gravel shoulder. The vehicle began to fishtail. "Hold on!" Eryn screamed. The van rolled over.

Dear God, not now—the children are with me! Lorie silently pleaded as the van rolled a second time. Immediately she heard a voice saying, "Don't be frightened. God is with you, and you will all be all right." She also had a vision of angels sitting on the children's laps, wrapping their arms around each little one. "An overwhelming sense of peace came over me," Lorie said, and she was able to relax even as the truck became airborne and flipped twice more, then came to a rest upright on a small hill.

The sudden silence was horrifying. Lorie was afraid to turn around and look, and instead fumbled for her cell phone. Where was it? Suddenly, everyone was crying. Cars around them were stopping. "Call an ambulance!" Lorie yelled, then turned to help the children.

Seeing everyone alive, she flew into action, pulling back two of the boys who were attempting to scramble through the broken windows, then passing four of the preschoolers to bystanders who had come to help. Eryn unbuckled Makayla, the screaming baby, from her car seat—she had probably saved Makayla from serious injury by wrapping herself around the baby as the van rolled. As the second-to-last child was removed, it suddenly occurred to Lorie that the van might roll again, but three-year-old Cody was still inside, too far for her reach. "But no one would let me crawl back to reach him," Lorie recalled. "I had to wait until the police arrived, and they got him out."

Wearily, Lorie climbed the hill. Good Samaritans had set all the children on blankets and were keeping them warm and safe. Lorie did a quick exam and discovered that four had escaped injury except for bruising from their seatbelts. The other three had glass cuts on their hands, but nothing more serious. As the ambulances arrived, she realized that she was covered in blood from a severed artery. She didn't know yet that she also had broken a vertebra. "A policeman told me later that when he saw the damage to my truck, he expected to be pulling bodies out of it," Lorie said. "No one could believe there weren't more serious injuries."

Later, Lorie discovered that her aunt, who lived seventy miles away, had been moved to get down on her knees and pray for a relative who was traveling. The feeling came upon her at 3:30 PM, the exact time Lorie's truck began to roll.

It was a miracle. But a few days later when her day care reopened, Lorie discovered she wasn't the only one to recognize it. "There were angels in our laps in the truck that day," a boy told Lorie matter-of-factly, then ran off to play. Before she could react, another child told her the same thing. Lorie remembered her vision: an angel in each child's lap protecting each little body and the calm voice that assured her everyone would survive. She had not mentioned this experience to anyone except Eryn, and yet the children knew. She gives thanks each day for this gift.

Storm at Sea

Ann Kovan

"I DON'T LIKE THIS WIND," I said to my friend Chris, watching the sails of our forty-foot catamaran twist and whip with each fierce gust. The waves had become increasingly choppy since sunset, and now the moon hid behind thick clouds. We'd been sailing together for nearly eight months, from San Francisco through the Panama Canal and on to the Bahamas. Now we were on our final open ocean leg to Beaufort, North Carolina. All day we'd had a gentle tailing breeze. Soon we were in a full-blown Nor'easter.

The boat hung off the back of each rolling wave before going into free fall and crashing down again. "We have to head for Charleston," I yelled to Chris. We had no charts to guide us but we had no choice.

We approached the harbor around midnight. We couldn't see a thing, so we radioed for help. Seconds later, a man on a little fishing skiff, barely larger than a rowboat, motored up. We followed his winding route all the way into the marina.

A week later, after repairing our ripped sails, we were ready to continue our journey. The daylight revealed the harbor to us. Unlit channel markers, derelict moored boats, a jagged, partially submerged jetty—a waterscape filled with hazards. Without the little skiff, we would have been sunk.

Only then did I wonder. There was no way a rescue vessel could have left shore and reached us so quickly after our call. And a tiny fishing boat had no business out in a Nor'easter in the middle of the night.

Angels from Interpol

Edward Grinnan

I AWOKE. OR REALLY, CAME to. I felt like a diver who had broken the surface of some murky, briny estuary. I had no idea how much time had elapsed. Days? I remembered visiting a church and how the blinding light through the windows had overwhelmed me. I had fragmentary memories of stumbling through Copenhagen, of an unpleasant encounter. Somehow I had managed to make it back here, where I'd been holed up for weeks, where no one knew who I was, which is how I wanted it.

From my vantage point on the floor I surveyed the hotel room. It was dusk, the long slow gloaming of a Scandinavian spring evening. May. This had all started with a spring festival while I was in the city on business for a Danish company I worked for at the time. *Started innocently enough*, I thought. *I thought I could handle just one.*

The room was a wreck. The bedclothes were heaped in a corner. Cigarette butts, overturned, overflowing ashtrays. In the middle of the floor was the phone, unplugged from the wall. Clothes were strewn about. Pages of the *International Herald Tribune*. Room service plates mostly untouched. There was no telling how long since I'd eaten. Days, probably. Empty bottles everywhere, especially those miniatures you get in hotel mini bars.

The window was open, the standard-issue diaphanous hotel curtains undulating languidly in a raw, wet updraft; the cold a relief on my face, half of which I feared bore the imprint of the rug. I could not remember opening the window, but I had a good idea why. We were twenty-one floors up. A straight, unimpeded plunge.

I needed to get myself a drink first, though I had no idea if I could keep it down. But my hands were shaking something awful. My whole body was shaking, and a terrible angst was beginning to boil up from the pit of my being, a crippling tide of panic and anxiety and dread.

I stood, unsteadily, and poured myself a drink, the bottle rattling against the glass due to my tremors, sounding almost like someone calling for a toast at a wedding. This was no toast. I wasn't even sure I could keep it down. This was purely medicinal. Without some alcohol in my system quick there was a good chance I could go into convulsions.

I lurched into the bathroom in case I couldn't keep the drink in, clenching my teeth so that if some of it did come surging up I might still be able to re-swallow it so the alcohol could get into my bloodstream and eventually my brain, where it would uncoil some of that terror. I was not new at the process, despite the fact that I hadn't yet turned thirty. I leaned over the toilet bowl to be ready just in case and was horrified to notice it was full of blood and bits of my stomach lining, and I vaguely recalled an attack of the dry heaves sometime earlier.

I hit the flushing mechanism with my foot and nearly fell over, caught my balance by grabbing the sink and found myself face to face with a ravaged visage in the mirror that took me a moment to recognize as mine.

I saw a depraved doppelgänger staring back at me, seeming like he could almost leap out and wrestle me out that window. This was the me that had just thrown away two years of hard-earned sobriety, a sobriety in which I thought I had discovered a personal relationship with a loving God to Whom I had relinquished my drinking and drugging and other manifold failings, to Whom I had given my life completely. But then one drink sitting dockside on a beautiful Danish evening had destroyed it all. How many days ago was that? How many weeks? Did it matter? I had changed hotels and dropped off the face of the earth, never returning from the business trip, contacting no one. I could only imagine what my mother was going through. She had already lost one son tragically.

Death was the ultimate. The end to shame, guilt, and remorse. I had been so hollowed by alcohol, they were the only emotions I could experience. Had I taken my will and life back from God, or had he thrown them back at me in disgust?

My feeling was beyond self-hatred, though it was surely that. I just no longer saw a reason for myself. This would not be an act of despair; it would be an act of reason. Suicide was never the final option. A drink was. I poured myself another one, supersized. I stared at the window. I had opened it for a reason and I knew what it was.

I pushed the window up. The drink was helping me feel a bit more back on my rails. I kicked off my shoes and straddled the sill, one leg hanging over the void, the other in tenuous contact with the floor. I leaned back, took a long pull from the glass and set it on my belly, feeling myself growing drowsy again, slumping ever so slightly out the window as the world faded. Maybe I should just let gravity make the decision.

I don't know how long I stayed poised between life and death, daring death to prevail and really quite indifferent to the outcome. I had entered that final petrified stage of hopelessness—the hopelessness of indifference.

I was utterly relaxed. I may have even drifted off before I was awakened by an insistent knocking at the door. My heart nearly exploded out of my chest, and I toppled to the floor, spilling alcohol everywhere.

"Are you in there?" a man's voice demanded. "Can you hear me?"

It was imperative they not kick the door in; I couldn't bear that on top of everything else, so I lurched over to the door and opened it a crack, keeping the chain on, and peered out.

A Motorcycle Miracle

Joan Wester Anderson

JOHN WAS A TEENAGER, RAISED in a very religious family. But he was more interested in hot cars and pretty girls. "My faith was very superficial," he said, "consisting mostly of a strict adherence to the rules, except when my parents weren't looking."

Shortly after getting his driver's license, John landed a well-paying job at a local grocery store chain. Soon he talked his dad into letting him buy a motorcycle. "Now, my independence was complete," John explained. "I earned my own money. I was buying my own vehicle. I felt like an adult." (And at six feet tall and 250 pounds, he certainly looked like one.)

So one day when John's mother forbade him from visiting his girlfriend after school, he was immediately rebellious. "I'm going, and nothing you can say or do will change my mind!" he shouted. His mother, stunned, began to cry. John had never defied her. But now her son was storming out the back door. "I'll be home by ten!" he shouted over his shoulder.

After school, John went to his girlfriend's house in a nearby town about thirty minutes away. The teens spent the evening together watching television. "I was so wrapped up in her that I paid no attention to the time," John said. Finally at 9:45, he headed home. But getting home normally took a half hour. To shave time off his drive, John decided to take a shortcut across a highway closed for construction. Veering around the yellow-and-black striped barricades, John sped up to about seventy miles per hour. A few moments later, he lost control, and the motorcycle began to flip.

"Time seemed to slow to a crawl," John recalled. "I hit the pavement, head first, and tumbled down the highway, head over heels. I remember seeing the moon pass my knees. And as I rolled to a stop, I remember the extreme silence of the night." Clothes torn, John was bleeding from head to toe and could barely move. He was also in the middle of nowhere, on a detoured highway, with no hope of traffic coming by. Would he die, he wondered hazily, before the road crews discovered him the next morning?

"As I lay there drifting in and out of consciousness, I saw two very bright lights approaching," John said. "It was a car, and I knew I needed to stop it." Shakily, John stumbled to his feet, stood swaying in the middle of the road and waved his arms for a moment, then fell again onto the pavement. But the driver had apparently seen him, for the car slowed, then stopped. It was a recreational vehicle.

A man stepped out of the RV and quickly assessed the situation. He lifted John's huge motorcycle to the side of the road, then easily picked John up in his arms, and carried him to the side of his RV. How did he have so much strength? John couldn't concentrate. Everything seemed to be happening a million miles away.

He passed out until they reached his girlfriend's house. "Her surprised mother opened the door, and the man carried me inside and laid me down on their couch," John said. He faded again.

Later at the hospital, John and his mother heard an amazing story. His girlfriend's mother explained that with hardly a word of explanation, the stranger had deposited John on their couch, and while the women were caring for John, he disappeared.

The incident was a turning point for John. He became far more serious about his behavior, his respect for his mother, and especially his faith in God. "I have thought about that accident over the years," he said, "and have found several things that I cannot explain.

"For example, how did I escape a high-speed crash with only minor cuts and abrasions? Why was the stranger driving on a barricaded road? How could he be strong enough to move the motorcycle, and to easily carry me in his arms? How did he know where my girlfriend lived? How did he leave without the women noticing? Finally, why didn't the man stick around and see how I was doing?"

Perhaps the man already knew John would be fine. "I believe in angelic beings, although I am skeptical about the popular view of their interventions," John said. "But I can't help but wonder if my rescuer that night was an angel."

Sarge

Walter Summers

How did a guy like me wind up in what was then known as Saigon, Vietnam, in 1966? Looking out my dirty hotel window one evening I still wasn't sure. There was a war being fought in the jungles north of us. But that wasn't what brought me here. I was here for the paycheck. I was hired by an American firm contracted by the US Navy for construction work. My skills as an engineer were in demand.

Right away I knew I did not like Saigon. It was hot, dirty, and confusing. We engineers lived in a fleabag hotel called the Mondial. Mainly, I kept to myself and stayed inside the hotel. The more experienced guys warned us not to wander off alone, especially after dark. There were horror stories of American businessmen or contractors such as ourselves disappearing down alleyways and never being heard from again. The streets certainly didn't look welcoming with their unfamiliar shops, signs I couldn't read, and soldiers walking around with guns.

I miss America, I thought as I gazed down onto the busy street below. Nothing—not the job nor the money—seemed worth this kind of loneliness. I missed my family and friends back in the States. I felt miles away from anything friendly. But still, I had to eat. I tied my shoelaces and double-locked the hotel door behind me. It was time for my daily trek out into the streets of Saigon for dinner.

Once I'd had a decent meal I walked back to the hotel. I strolled slower than I usually did, taking in some of the knickknacks being sold at the various carts around the plaza by the hotel. *These folks aren't so different from me*, I thought. *I should try to enjoy the adventure.* It was good to be out and about. At least, surrounded by people, I felt a little less alone.

Then I realized the sky had gotten dark. Sundown. How many times was I warned to get back to the hotel before dark? I walked more quickly toward the Mondial. *Lord,* I prayed, *if Your angels exist, I'd love to have one of them protect me now.*

A cycle-powered pedicab blew past me, and I yelled after him, hoping for a faster trip home. He slowed to a stop. "Hello," I said. "Hotel Mondial." The cabbie nodded and started pedaling off. Something didn't seem right though. He was taking a strange route back to the hotel. The cabbie spun the pedicab into a very dark and deserted alleyway. There was another man in the alleyway already. He nodded in recognition at the pedicab driver. My worst fears about Saigon were coming true. I was trapped! I leapt out of the pedicab, but the men cornered me up against a brick wall in the alley. I was alone, in the dark. My two would-be assailants blocked the only exit.

As they moved toward me, I could make out a third figure, shrouded in shadows, coming up behind them. He towered over the both of them. *Oh no*, I thought. *Three against one. I'll never make it. I'm going to be the subject of one of those horror stories new guys get told.*

When they stepped out of the shadows, I saw the towering figure wore a US uniform with master sergeant stripes. "Sarge?" I whispered. The two assailants wheeled around, just now seeing the hulking soldier behind them. They froze in their tracks. I skittered over to him. We walked out of the alley and toward the Mondial. The two muggers didn't dare follow. Never was I so happy to see that hotel. "Thanks, Sarge," I said when we reached the glass doors. He said nothing in return. I noticed he wasn't wearing a sidearm. That was unheard of. And since when do master sergeants walk around Saigon after dark? Alone? I put my hand on the door and turned around. "Hey, thanks again…" I froze with my mouth half open. The soldier was gone. I looked back down the way we came, but the towering figure was nowhere to be seen.

As I dragged my weary body through the lobby of the Mondial, I remembered the prayer I'd made earlier that night. The Lord does have His ministering angels, and they do help those in need.

The Rescue Rain

Douglas Scott Clark

BEARS WERE COMMON IN THE Smoky Mountains come fall. But when one of them started raiding our family's beehives, I grabbed my rifle and cow horn and headed up Chestnut Mountain with my hunting dogs to track him down. The dogs picked up a scent in the huckleberry bushes. I ran after them, determined to keep up. Soon we were a mile deeper into the mountains than I'd wanted to venture that morning.

I sat down on a log to catch my breath. I could hear the dogs barking as they trailed the bear along the far ridge line. Then I heard something else—distant thunder. I turned to the west, shading my eyes from the sun. A long line of yellow-gray clouds filled the sky. Lightning streaks danced down from the clouds in thin, branching threads. "Dry lightning," I said. "There sure ain't any rain in that mess."

The section of Smokys where my family lived hadn't gotten rain in more than seven weeks. The forest was as dry as I'd ever seen it. At sixteen, I knew a dry forest plus dry lightning was a recipe for disaster. I didn't want any bear that badly. Not even one threatening my family. I stood up and blew on my old cow horn. The sound sent a few birds up into the sky and brought the dogs running.

They gathered around me like eager children, tails wagging, tongues hanging out. "We'll go down by the stream so you all can get a drink," I said. "Then we'll cut across the mountains and head for home."

At the stream I filled my canteen. Then I hitched my rifle on my shoulder and called, "Let's go home!" We started climbing. As we came up over the top of Chestnut Mountain I got a chance to observe the storm more closely. It had intensified since I saw it in the valley. It was dangerous, yes, but it was also beautiful. Crooked lightning forked from one cloud to another, making them glow in a mixture of yellows, blues, and whites.

The dogs disappeared ahead of me. They'd make it home long before me. I stopped for a sip from my canteen.

Crash! Thunder boomed above my head, so loud the ground reverberated under my feet. A flash of lightning bleached out the sky. My whole body tingled. I looked up into the heavens. *What is that?*

A bright, luminous sphere descended from the clouds. I'd never seen anything like it. I was terrified. The phantom ball hovered a few inches above the ground, then moved around the mountain—leaving a trail of flames in its wake.

Fear gripped me. I was too scared to run. I could only watch in horror as the sphere spread fire along the mountain—right across the path to the other side and home. Once it had cut off my escape, the ball disintegrated before my eyes.

At last my legs started working. I raced off in the opposite direction, back to the creek where we'd stopped to get water. The flames advanced behind me, moving fast over the ground. I remembered an old story my father told me. "I was only a little boy," Daddy had said. "I was walking home with your granddad one stormy night when a ball of fire came out of the clouds. It traveled over the valley, right into an abandoned cabin. A second later the cabin was completely consumed by flames."

Daddy had seen the mysterious fire too. He'd even discovered its name—ball lightning. *Daddy and I can have a long talk about it when I get home*, I thought as I reached the stream. *If I make it home!*

The tiny stream was no firebreak. At best it would be a temporary stopgap to slow the fire. My chances of outrunning the flames on foot ranged from slim to hopeless to none. I dropped my rifle into the water. Normally leaving that rifle behind would be unthinkable. Now, with the heat of the fire bearing down on me, I just couldn't carry the extra weight. I could only hope I'd live long enough to retrieve it again. I looked over my shoulder as I laid it down. The flames had topped the crest of Chestnut Mountain. The race was on!

I pumped my arms and legs and kept my eyes on the far ridge. I was young and athletic, but the mountain was steep. My breath came in short, raspy gasps. A sharp, stabbing pain pierced my side. But I couldn't stop. Ahead, at the top of the next ridge, was a large outcropping of rock. If I could make it there, I thought, I might have a chance. If the rocks could provide protection from the fire.

I ran, I stumbled. I crawled when I had to. Finally I reached the stone formation. I crawled into the center of the rocks and collapsed. I looked down at the valley around me. The forest was an inferno. The fire had followed the natural terrain of the hollows, completely surrounding my little island of stone, and the flames were getting closer. I huddled in a crevice and covered myself with my coat. The air around me got hotter as the flames closed in. *It's like hiding in an oven,* I thought. *I just might be roasted alive here.*

My legs prickled as the heat penetrated my trousers. I tucked my legs up as close as I could to my body. Thoughts of home rushed into my mind. My mother, my father, my sisters, my little brother, Buddy Earl. But that wasn't the home I was going to now. I was headed to my home with God. If it was my time, I had to accept it.

I threw back my coat and raised my arms to the sky. "Please, dear Lord, accept me into Your presence and take care of my family!"

I held my breath. I heard a strange sound, like the fluttering of a thousand wings beating together.

Then came the rain. Not a light rain like a shower on a spring day or a summer's afternoon, but a great deluge. The skies opened up and water poured down in a torrent. I ducked my head for fear of drowning in it. The rocks around me sizzled and steamed when the blessed rain touched them.

When the downpour stopped, and I could raise my head, I saw the valley around me blackened and charred, but safe once again. On shaky legs I made my way back to the stream to retrieve my rifle, then down the slope toward home. I opened the back door and found Mama at the kitchen sink. I'd never been so glad to see her.

"What happened to you?" Mama asked, frowning at my still-dripping clothes. "How'd you get so wet?"

"Caught in the downpour," I said.

"Downpour?" Mama said. "We didn't get any rain here. This side of the mountain didn't see a drop."

Guess my guardian angel knew where that rain was needed most.

Lifeguard on Duty?

Danita Cahill

A DAY OF SWIMMING! MY friend Melinda and I giggled as we splashed in the swimming hole of the Siletz River in Siletz, Oregon. Her mother and uncle waved from the bank.

We weren't the only ones who'd decided to make the best of a sunny summer afternoon—the swimming hole was crowded with adults horsing around in the water and dangling their feet over the edge of the rocky Siletz riverbank. One couple in particular caught my attention. They were sitting on the rockiest slope, and the man was wearing swim trunks. I'd never seen a man so muscular! To a nine-year-old girl like me, he looked like the circus strong man.

"Come on!" Melinda called as we splashed. "Let's swim out a ways."

"Okay," I said, "follow me!" I dog-paddled furiously into deeper water. I thought I was a decent swimmer, even if my dog-paddling and poor imitation of the breaststroke made up my entire swimming repertoire.

Melinda and I paddled about happily until I felt a suction pulling at my feet. It was as if something was trying to drag me under. My mind raced for explanations: Eels? Giant leeches? The Loch Ness monster?

Whatever it was I wanted to get away from it—fast. But when I tried to tighten up my dog-paddle the invisible creature pulled at my feet even harder, like a great underwater vacuum. I didn't know anything about undercurrents, or how quickly one could pull a swimmer beneath the water and downriver. I just knew I was in trouble. "Help!" I yelled.

Water poured over my chin and into my mouth. I gagged and spit. Melinda tried to help me. In my panic I grabbed at the first thing I could—Melinda's hair. I dunked her under.

"Help!" she screamed. "You're drowning me!"

Melinda's sister and her uncle ran from shore and swam out to me. Now I was truly desperate. I clawed and scratched at their faces and arms, trying to attach myself to something solid. The undercurrent pulled at them. They were no match for its vice grip. They couldn't save me! I was so scared, I barely knew what was happening.

All I knew was I couldn't fight any longer. My arms stopped flailing. I relaxed my head. I sank below the surface and began a slow descent to the bottom. I watched the last of my air bubbles float to the surface, where the sun was turning the water a beautiful green hue. *I'm going to die*, I thought.

Just then an arm wrapped tightly about my waist. My body was yanked up through the water. In seconds I was breathing in air and looking into the face of my rescuer. It was the circus strong man! From the riverbank! He flung all eighty pounds of me over his shoulder like a sack of feathers.

When we got to shore everyone was waiting: clapping, holding their breaths, or sighing in relief. I opened my mouth to thank my rescuer, but when I tried to make a sound I could only wince and clutch at my raw throat. The strong man laid me down on the dry riverbank, and Melinda's family covered me with a blanket.

"Are you all right, Danita?" someone asked. "Thank God that man was here today," someone else said. I lay on my side, coughing up water. Between coughs, my eyes searched the crowd for the strong man. But he was nowhere to be seen.

As soon as I was able to stand, we all got in the car to go home. On the ride back my mind was full of questions: Who was the strong man? How was he able to save me when no one else could? And why hadn't the man stayed around for me to thank him?

Throughout my childhood I thought often about that day on the river, and when I grew up and got married I told my husband about the experience. "Have you ever considered that the strong man could have been your guardian angel?" he asked.

"But I saw him on the beach," I said. "Everyone did."

"He was on that beach for a reason," my husband said. "Don't you think God put him there?"

A man acting as a guardian angel? I'd never thought about it that way before. Many people tried to save me and failed. Luckily there was a man on the river that day, with the strength of an angel.

Mountaintop Miracle

James L. Garlow & Keith Wall

LEROY LANE FELT UNCOMFORTABLE, BUT he kept driving—higher and higher up a mountain road east of Phoenix, Arizona. Leroy and his family had recently moved to the Phoenix area so he could recover from the allergies that plagued him in their native Michigan. Now on this sunny, ninety-degree Saturday, he was taking his family on an adventure—an exploration of the country surrounding their new home. For a self-described flatlander, however, driving a big blue Chevy van to an elevation past fifteen hundred feet on a narrow, rock-strewn road was nerve-racking.

Leroy had to concentrate hard on every switchback as the Chevy climbed. Just twelve inches past the edge of the asphalt, sometimes on both sides, the road fell away sharply, revealing deep canyons far below. They were so close to the sky Leroy almost felt he could reach out and shake hands with God.

"This is so weird," said thirteen-year-old Mike, looking out the backseat window at the brown, treeless mountain and barren landscape below.

"It's ugly," said his brother, nine-year-old Matt.

Fran, Leroy's supportive wife, didn't comment from her viewpoint in the front passenger seat. But Leroy could tell from the expression on her face that she was equally unimpressed. Their outing was off to a less-than-stellar start.

A moment later, Leroy saw a chance to salvage the situation. Up ahead was a small metal sign pointing left. It read, Mormon Flat Dam. Leroy took the turn.

"What are we doing?" Fran asked.

"We're going to see Mormon Flat Dam," Leroy answered. "It's an adventure!"

The adventure included one of the roughest roads Leroy had ever seen. Rocks the size of footballs littered the trail. He slowed to a crawl, but the Chevy still bounced around like a ball in a pinball game. Finally, the Lanes reached a flat area about fifty feet long and fifteen feet wide that marked the end of the trail.

Sheer rock walls bordered the deserted "parking lot" on the right and straight ahead. To the left was a narrow ramp that dropped to another flat area twenty-five feet below. On both sides of the ramp and beyond the lower flat area was a drop-off of hundreds of feet.

The Lanes got out of the van to look around. They discovered another couple who had driven to the lower level in a small station wagon. They also heard the sound of rushing water, but there was no sign of the dam.

"We must have missed a turnoff someplace," Leroy surmised.

"Dad, let's go home," Mike said. "There's nothing here."

Leroy took a last look at their forlorn spot. There was no trail, no marker pointing a way to the dam. He had to admit defeat.

"Okay," he finally said. "Back in the van."

Leroy realized the "parking lot" didn't offer enough room to turn the van around. But he could see the ramp in his rearview mirror. If he could back down the ramp a few feet, it would provide the extra space he needed to maneuver the van and point it toward the direction they had come. After turning the steering wheel, Leroy inched the Chevy back toward the ramp. He felt the rear wheels descend. But he still needed more room to complete the turn. He backed up some more. Suddenly, Leroy felt the van's front left side slump. *Uh-oh.* He rolled down his window and peered down.

The Chevy's left front tire was dangling over open space. Leroy cracked the door open to make sure he wasn't seeing things. Sure enough, the view down went on and on. Suddenly, the Lanes were in an extremely precarious position.

"Everybody stay calm," he said—as much to himself as to his family. He considered the predicament a moment. They were more than fifty miles from home. They were in mostly deserted mountains. His Chevy now blocked the couple in the station wagon below. No doubt about it—they were in big trouble.

"Okay, everybody get out on the right side," Leroy said in a quiet, firm voice. "Get clear of the van."

His family quickly obeyed. Leroy hadn't been wearing his seatbelt. Now he strapped it on and slowly straightened his wheels. He shifted into drive and attempted to inch forward. The Chevy had rear-wheel drive, but the back wheels couldn't find traction on the ramp's slippery rock surface. They were stuck. Leroy climbed out the right passenger door to take a closer look.

Fran and the couple with the station wagon joined him. Leroy shook his head. "How are we going to get this thing out of here?"

"Well, we could push," the other man offered. "We can help you."

"Thanks," Leroy said. "I guess it's worth a try."

Leroy crawled through the right doorway and back into the driver's seat. Fran and the other couple took positions at the back of the van. Leroy put his foot on the gas pedal. But on every attempt, the rear tires simply spun in place. The Chevy didn't move. "I think you need to give it more gas!" the man called from the ramp.

"Yeah, I think you're right," Leroy answered. "We need more horsepower." The two boys joined the team at the back of the van.

When they were ready, Leroy floored it. He stopped when he heard a thud. Wondering what had happened, Leroy scrambled out the right door again. Everyone was gathered around Fran, who stood there gritting her teeth and examining her leg. Leroy looked, too, and saw a large area on her thigh quickly growing black and blue. When he'd punched the gas, the spinning right rear tire had found just enough traction to grab one of the football-sized stones and hurl it into Fran's leg.

"Fran, I am so sorry," Leroy told her. He felt terrible. He was also more worried than ever. Fran was able to stand but was clearly in pain. Her leg didn't seem broken, but what if her injury was more serious than it appeared? How were they going to get medical attention? Their adventure was turning into a nightmare. Leroy didn't know what to do, but he didn't want his family to know that. He got back into the driver's seat as if he had a plan in mind. Then he closed his eyes and bowed his head. "Lord," he prayed out loud, "I need your help now!"

Leroy opened his eyes—and was shocked to see an old Buick LeSabre rattling toward him. It moved within a few feet of the van's front bumper and stopped. Both front doors flew open, and out stepped two characters that Leroy would have avoided on any other occasion. They were big men, with unshaven faces and dark, scruffy hair that fell to their shoulders. Both wore blue jeans, sleeveless T-shirts, and red bandanas on their heads. They looked like they belonged on Harleys instead of inside a Buick.

"You guys need help," the driver said. It was a statement, not a question. Leroy wasn't sure if he trusted these men. Their expressions weren't menacing, but they weren't smiling either. Their look was businesslike—they were there to do a job. No matter their intentions, Leroy couldn't deny the dire circumstances. "We certainly do," he responded. The Buick's driver positioned himself at the front of the van on Leroy's side while the other man moved to the Chevy's rear.

"Turn your wheel to the right," the driver instructed. That didn't make sense to Leroy. But even as he doubted, he felt a sense of calm and assurance wash over him. He somehow understood that these men knew what they were doing and would help.

"Okay, back down slowly," the driver said. "Easy now." Leroy did as he was told.

"Brake!" called the man in back a moment later. For the next few minutes, the men gave Leroy instructions on how to maneuver the van. They spoke in quiet, confident voices, never contradicting each other. Leroy had the sense they'd done this many times before.

Soon Leroy had all four wheels on the ramp and was backing all the way down to the flat area below. As soon as he was on level ground, he turned his head behind him to make sure his family and the other couple were safe and accounted for. A second later, Leroy turned his head forward again. He wanted to thank the two men who had appeared out of nowhere and saved him from a frightening scenario. But the men were gone. Leroy blinked. *Where did those guys go?* he thought. *How did they do that?*

Leroy's mind raced. The two men had been standing close to the van. Even if they'd somehow scampered up the ramp and out of sight in the moment Leroy turned his head, where was the Buick? It would have taken the same maneuvering down the ramp that Leroy had just completed for them to turn around. Even if they had backed out the way they came in—which would have been dangerous and foolhardy—Leroy would have heard them bumping over the rocks through his open window. Leroy ran up the ramp, his eyes scanning the area for clues, but there were none. The men and the LeSabre had vanished.

God sent them, Leroy thought. *He sent helpers at just the right moment to keep the four of us from harm. I have just witnessed heaven's angels.*

Ocean Guides

Kristina Cunningham

UNCLE PETER AND I HEADED down the wooden walkway toward the ocean with our beach towels in hand.

"Too bad no one else wanted to join us!" he said. We'd left the rest of the family back at the picnic tables, but there was no way I was going to miss the chance for a swim.

My feet sank into the warm sand. I wiggled my toes. I was feeling good. Energized. Healthy. Able to take care of myself. That was certainly a change, because for so long every day had been a struggle. As a teenager, I'd developed a variety of illnesses. My ailments worsened and multiplied as I entered adulthood: with my thyroid and immune system, migraines, chronic fatigue, and vitamin deficiencies. As my body weakened and my pain intensified, I relied more on God. He got me through the hardest days.

Now I was feeling better than I had in years. More than ready for a swim! I spread my towel out on the beach and looked out to sea. There wasn't a cloud in the sky. In the distance, seagulls perched on the jagged rocks by the break wall that protected an old fishing pier. *Like a scene from a postcard*, I thought.

"Looks like we have the beach to ourselves," Uncle Peter said. "And on this beautiful day!"

I ran down to the shoreline. The ankle-deep water was choppy, and it sent sand and broken seashells crashing against my feet. It was rougher than I had expected. But the salty ocean breeze felt good against my face, and it would be nice to cool off. I wasn't going to let a few waves spoil my day at the beach.

"Let's wade out past the white caps," I said. "The water's always calmer once you put a little distance between yourself and the shore."

We fought through the waves until the water was up to our waistlines. Instead of getting calmer, the sea got even rougher. Some of the waves were taller than I was, and the undertow made it hard to stand still. I tried to paddle back to shore, but I couldn't fight the waves. I looked back at Uncle Peter.

A wave crashed over me and knocked me down. My body tossed and turned beneath the surface of the water. Salty seawater filled my mouth. The sea swirled around me. I couldn't see. I couldn't breathe. My chest tightened as I ran out of air. I was helpless again. Only this time I was struggling underwater instead of being sick in bed.

Finally my head broke through the surface. I saw my uncle in the distance, closer to shore. I tried to make my way toward him, but my muscles were weak compared to the might of the ocean. I couldn't even catch enough breath to call for help.

A wave crashed over my head. The undertow pulled me farther out to sea. Every time my head popped up, a wave came to beat me down. Each one pushed me closer to the break wall that protected the pier. What if a strong one threw me into it? All those years God had helped me fight—was it just to let me drown here? *Dear God, please help me! I still need you! I may not be sick anymore, but I'm not strong enough for this!* I struggled to swim, but the power of the ocean was too strong. Another wave. I went under.

Then, instead of the dull rush of the undertow around my ears, I heard the wind and the waves of the beach. I opened my eyes. I was no longer near the rocks. In fact, I was much closer to shore than I had been just a moment before. Practically on the sand. *How did I get here?*

I touched my feet to the ocean floor. Gasping for breath, I dragged myself to the beach. I collapsed next to Uncle Peter on the dry sand. We lay there for a few minutes, struggling to catch our breath.

Finally, I could speak. "I don't know how I got out of that," I said. "One second I was being pulled toward the rocks by the pier. The next I was near the shore."

"All I know is, you were being pulled farther from me," he said. "Then, you were on the beach. Are you all right?"

"Yes, I think so." *But how?*

Uncle Peter and I made our way back to the others. We tried to tell them what had happened. "It's a mystery how I escaped the water and rocks," I said. As the words left my lips, an image came to my mind. I saw myself back in the ocean. I was not alone. Two bright white figures stood on either side of me. The waves roared, but they were not affected by the fury of the water. Each figure took an elbow, and together they guided me toward the beach. *Two angels pulled me to safety*, I thought.

How had I not seen it before? It was God all along. He had seen me struggling, and sent angels to move me away from the dangerous water. Tears sprung to my eyes as I realized the enormity of what He had done. I had relied on Him for strength and guidance when I was ill, and He was still there for me. Every minute of every day. He always would be. Sick or strong, I could rely on God to help me ride out the waves.

CHAPTER 2

Messengers of Love

Pennies from Heaven

Beaver Brown

I WAS AT THE BUS stop, heading home after a long, busy night waiting tables at a steak house, when I realized I'd left behind my money pouch, with seventy dollars of tips in it. I couldn't afford to lose a night's pay.

I ran back into the restaurant. There was no sign of my money. Just imagine you had the night off, I told myself. I'd try to forget about it.

The next night was even busier than the one before. I was already waiting on five tables at once, when an elderly couple, both with snow-white hair, sat down in my section. No matter how harried I was, I made sure to give them the best service I could. After their meal, I brought their check, thanked them for their patience and rushed off to greet my next customers.

The couple had left the table by the time I picked up their check. *This isn't right*, I thought, counting the money they'd left for me. There was much more here than their fifty-five dollar check. Way too much for a tip. I counted it out. One hundred and twenty-five dollars!

Quickly, I turned around to look for the couple. They'd left the restaurant. I ran to the front door, but they weren't outside. Finally, I went to the hostess. "Did you see that elderly couple you sat in my section leave?"

"What elderly couple?" the hostess said. "You were so busy, we didn't seat anyone in your section, until just now."

A Surprising Visit

Diantha Stensrud

COULD IT REALLY BE MORE than twenty years since my brother, Patrick, got married? Looking at the wedding album in his living room, it seemed like yesterday. "I always loved that blue dress you wore," Patrick's wife, Melissa, said, pointing to a picture of me in a tea-length gown with puffy sleeves.

"There's Mom and me dancing," said Patrick, turning the page.

"I almost expect to see Dad," I said. "Even though he couldn't be there."

"You know who else it makes me think about?" Patrick said. "Winnie and Fred. Do you remember them?"

"I'll never forget them," I said.

We hadn't talked about the couple in years, but hearing their names brought me back to that spring of 1983. My father had been diagnosed with terminal lung cancer. He lived at home with Mom, who was a registered nurse. She cared for him with the help of hospice nurses. That way Dad could still enjoy some things he loved. From a hospital bed set up in the living room, Dad could talk to Mom, read, or play solitaire. Some days he felt strong enough to play his organ. Dad was a professional musician and never liked to be far away from his Hammond B3.

I visited Dad in June. We chatted about Patrick's upcoming wedding, which Dad insisted go on as planned. Before I left he wrote me a check for a new dress.

"Look your best, kid," he said as he handed it to me. His voice, once so rich and familiar, was already so weak he barely made any sound at all.

Dad wanted us to focus on Patrick and Melissa, but all I could think about was him. We'd lost so much of him already: the brightness in his eyes, the sound of his voice. I couldn't remember the last time I'd heard that belly laugh of his. What I wouldn't have given to hear it again.

I chose a tea-length silk blue gown and took it to Dad's house to model it for him. He gave me a thumbs-up from his hospital bed. I'd just finished changing when the doorbell rang. A couple I'd never seen before stood on the stoop. "I'm Winnie," the woman said. Her smile was so natural and friendly it was clear she smiled a lot. "This is my husband, Fred. We just moved into the neighborhood."

I shook hands with them both.

"We had to meet whoever made all the beautiful music," said Fred.

I introduced them to Mom and Dad. Winnie complimented Dad on his playing. Within moments I saw Winnie's smile reflected on Dad's face. Winnie and Fred were still there when I left, chatting with Dad about music. They seemed to have no trouble hearing his voice despite how weak it was. In fact, his voice sounded a little stronger since they'd come. "I'll see you soon," I said, kissing Dad good-bye.

"Winnie likes cards as much as your dad," Mom told me a few days later. "The two of them played for hours yesterday. Much longer than the other nurses or I can take. Dad absolutely loved it."

Patrick, Melissa, and I got used to seeing Winnie at the house. Sometimes she was with Fred, sometimes she came by herself. "Your dad's telling me about his amazing career," Winnie said one afternoon as I came in. Dad was at the organ taking her song requests. "I'm a nurse, myself."

Dad shrugged modestly, but his blue eyes sparkled, the way they used to before he got sick. "Winnie sure has a great effect on Dad," I told Mom as we made coffee in the kitchen. "I didn't know she was a nurse."

"Even if she wasn't a nurse she'd still be a big help," Mom said. "Have you noticed the difference in Dad when he's with her?"

"It's like he lights up whenever she's with him," I said.

Out in the living room, Dad laughed. The great big belly laugh I hadn't heard in ages.

"Winnie's the only one who gets him to laugh like that," Mom said. "The other day she arrived at the door wearing a red clown nose she'd made out of a ping-pong ball. We thought we'd never stop laughing!"

That evening I walked Winnie back to the complex of town homes where she and Fred lived. "I can't get over hearing Dad laugh again," I said. "I missed it so much."

"Laughter is the most important medicine," said Winnie. "I told your brother—find something to laugh about every single day."

"That can be pretty hard to do sometimes," I said quietly.

Winnie squeezed my shoulder. "I know it can be, with your father so sick. But humor keeps the soul alive and well, even in the darkest times. So I always try to find something to laugh about. Even if it's at myself!"

Winnie grinned at me, and I burst out laughing. "All right, I guess I could try that," I promised her.

She gave me a hug at the door of her town home. "I'd invite you in, but our furniture hasn't arrived yet."

"You don't have any furniture?" I said. "That must be difficult."

"Our things are on their way," Winnie said, cheerful as always. "There's no rush."

I said good night, marveling at the joy Winnie seemed to find in everything. And the way she made our family feel that joy too, even at a time like this. Now when I talked about Patrick and Melissa's wedding I was able to look forward to it. "Maybe Dad will be able to make it to the wedding after all," I said to Patrick one afternoon.

But it wasn't to be. Dad died at home, surrounded by family and friends. We gathered at the house after the funeral. The space where Dad's hospital bed had once sat was empty. "Winnie and Fred arranged for it to be taken out," Melissa said. "Wasn't that nice?"

"They're a miracle," Patrick said. "How many nights did Winnie sit up with Dad so Mom could sleep?"

Across the room Winnie chatted with Mom. For the first time that day, she was almost smiling. *Leave it to Winnie to give Mom something to laugh about today*, I thought. Patrick's wedding went on as planned, just as Dad had wanted. I wore my blue dress. I even found things to smile about, like remembering Dad saying, "Look your best, kid." I wasn't ready to actually laugh much yet, but keeping on the lookout for happy things reminded me there was still joy in the world, even without Dad. Winnie had taught me that.

A few days after the wedding I drove over to see Mom. I brought flowers for Winnie. "Even if she's got no furniture, she can still have flowers," I told Mom. I had no doubt Winnie would appreciate the bright colors. I walked over to the town house and knocked on the door. "Winnie?" I called. "It's Di. Are you in?"

There was no answer. *They must be out*, I thought. Then I noticed a sign on the sidewalk outside the house: Condo for Lease. I hadn't noticed that sign when I'd walked Winnie home. Was there some sort of mistake? Were Winnie and Fred moving away already? I walked over to the manager's office. "That condo says it's for lease," I said, pointing to Winnie and Fred's place. "Did the couple there move already? Winnie and Fred?"

"I don't know anyone by that name," he said. "That unit's been empty for two months at least. Nobody's even asked about leasing it, much less moved in!"

Twenty years later, looking at the old photo album, Patrick, Melissa, and I went silent, each pondering the mystery of Winnie and Fred. We never saw or heard from them again. "We don't even have pictures," I said. "It's as if they never existed. But everything would have been so different without them."

"They were angels," Patrick said. "They came to help Dad, and they helped all the rest of us too."

Was Patrick right? I guess I don't know for sure. But when I think of angels now, I picture them wearing red clown noses. That certainly gives me something to laugh about.

The Silent Chaplain

Marlene J. Chase

BOUTS OF PNEUMONIA AND SEVERE asthma had dogged our child since birth—but never like this. Sitting in the hospital waiting room, my husband and I didn't know if he'd survive the night. We'd been at Grandma's house when his lungs suddenly seized up. Epinephrine injections didn't help. Now he was on a ventilator.

The nurse checked in on us from time to time to see if we needed anything. Otherwise, we were alone with our worries. Until a chaplain entered the room. I expected him to say the obligatory prayers, wish us well, and move on to others in need. And indeed, he sat across from us, leaned forward and bowed his head. But he said nothing.

Perhaps he doesn't want to intrude, I thought. Still, I was grateful for his presence. His silent prayer was comforting. I tried to sleep. Each time I briefly opened my eyes, I saw the chaplain there, deep in meditation.

After a restless night, the first rays of dawn finally crept through the window blinds. The nurse entered the room. "Your son is out of danger," she said. "He's going to be fine!" My husband and I raced to his bedside.

Afterward, we asked the nurse how we could thank the hospital chaplain for waiting with us so long during the night.

"The chaplain?" the nurse said, puzzled. "He's on vacation."

"So who was sitting in the waiting room with us?" I asked.

"I checked on you all night," the nurse said. "You were alone."

A Secret for Five

Pam Zollman

I KNEW A SECRET. ONLY three people—maybe four—knew this secret: me; my husband, Bill; his secretary, Jill; and maybe Jill's husband.

And what was that secret?

Bill, my husband of nearly thirty years, wanted to divorce me and marry Jill.

Divorce is nothing new. It was going on even in Jesus' time. It wasn't even new to me. My mother has been married numerous times, divorcing my own father when I was two.

But I had never even envisioned myself divorced. Bill and I still held hands! Well, we did until February 14. That stopped after a romantic dinner at our favorite restaurant when he announced that he was moving out.

"Nothing you say or do will change my mind," Bill said.

Valentine's Day had always been important to Bill. While he might not always remember my birthday or our anniversary, he always remembered February 14th and made it special. He proposed to me on Valentine's Day, giving me flowers, treating me to dinner, and getting down on one knee after a stroll on the beach.

On the twenty-fifth anniversary of his proposal, he gave me a gold heart with a diamond at the center.

"Wear this always, and it will remind you of my love," he said.

That Valentine's night, I sat in shock, fingering the heart necklace I always wore and wondering how long our marriage had been a joke. I had not seen this coming.

I chose not to tell anyone about my husband's affair, especially not our two sons, because I was praying that Bill would change his mind. And if he did, I didn't want any of my friends or family members to hold his indiscretion against him. I loved him and was willing to forgive him. Plus, I think I was in denial. If I kept quiet about it, then it might not actually happen.

So a few days later when I went to the post office, the secret was still a secret.

When I got to the post office parking lot, I had about five minutes before the employees closed the doors. Another woman had pulled into the space next to mine. She struggled with three large boxes, obviously ready to mail.

"Let me help you," I said, taking a box.

"Thank you," she replied with a pronounced Hispanic accent. Her long black hair was pulled back at the sides and fastened with gold clips, and she wore an expensive dark green jacket and matching slacks, as if she'd just gotten off work. Large gold earrings matched her hair clips, and her makeup was perfect.

I, on the other hand, wore jeans and a sweater. My own dark hair was in a long braid down my back. In Houston, Texas, we have mild winters, so neither of us needed a coat.

She gripped a box in either arm and followed me into the post office, her heels clicking on the pavement. My tennis shoes scuffled. A postal employee locked the doors behind us.

As we joined the end of the short line, she asked me about postage.

"I am not from here," she said. A light citrus fragrance surrounded her. "I do not know how to mail these boxes."

"If you're not in a hurry for the packages to arrive, then it's pretty cheap to mail them. But if you want them to arrive by a certain date, then you'll have to pay more for first class or priority mail," I said, shifting her box so I was balancing it

on my hip. To the best of my knowledge, I explained the difference between the rates. "And the postal workers here are easy to work with. They'll help you."

As we moved up in line, she told me she was from Guatemala. "Our postal system is not very reliable."

"We complain about ours," I said, "but, overall, it works pretty well."

Two spots opened up at the counter, and I handed her the box I was carrying for her.

"Thank you," she said. "I appreciate your help."

I smiled. "No problem."

The woman behind the counter took my large brown envelope, weighed it, and stamped it. I paid for the postage and headed for the door. When the Guatemalan woman stepped away from the counter right behind me, I was surprised. I figured that it would take her longer because of the three boxes, but I was wrong. The postal worker was in a hurry to go home, I guessed.

Another employee unlocked the door and let us out.

"You've been so helpful," she said as we walked out together. "I would like to do something for you now."

"Oh goodness, no," I protested. "I didn't really do anything."

"Would you let me pray for you?" she asked.

"Pray for me?" That surprised me. As a Christian I had no problem with people praying for me, but a stranger had never offered to pray for me in a parking lot. I hesitated for only a moment.

"Sure," I said.

She stood in front of me and took both of my hands in hers. A charm bracelet jingled on her right wrist. Rings adorned several fingers, and her nails were painted pale pink. I closed my eyes as she began to pray.

"Heavenly Father, I lift up Pam—"

Pam. I didn't remember telling her my name . . . but, maybe I had?

"—and ask that You give her strength and courage to face her current situation."

My current situation? What?

"Give her and her two sons the guidance they'll need."

My two sons? I knew I'd never mentioned my family to her.

"And surround her with Your love during the divorce and afterward."

My eyes flew open, and I stared at her. Her eyes were still closed, and her face serene. How could she know any of this about me?

"Help her to know that the future holds great hope for her. Through Jesus Christ, I pray. Amen."

She opened her eyes and smiled at me, squeezing my hands.

I was so astonished I didn't know what to say.

She unhooked her charm bracelet and fastened it around my right wrist. "I want you to have this."

"Oh no," I said, "I couldn't possibly—"

She raised a hand, and I stopped speaking. "I want you to wear this. It will remind you of God's love for you."

I looked at the charm bracelet as my left hand fingered my necklace. Almost the exact words Bill had said to me five years earlier.

Eyeing my hand on the heart necklace, she shook her head.

"This isn't a promise like that one," she said. "This is God's promise to you. He loves you and wants you to be reminded of it, especially during the tough times that are ahead of you."

"How...how do you know these things?" I asked.

"Don't worry about that," she said with a smile. "Accept the gift and know that God loves you."

"Thank you," I said. I held my arm up and the charm bracelet jingled like tiny bells. "Could I have your name and phone number? I...I might want to talk to you again."

"Sure," she said and dug in her black purse. She scribbled her name and phone number on a torn piece of pink paper and handed it to me.

I wanted to be sure I wouldn't lose it, so I put it in the coin section of my wallet. "Thank you," I repeated.

She waved good-bye, got in her car, and drove off. I stood in the parking lot, staring at the bracelet.

The bracelet was silver, but was not an expensive piece of jewelry. The charms were set in three sets of threes. Each set had a leaping dolphin facing right, a star, and a leaping dolphin facing left. Nothing Christian about it. And yet, I felt special wearing it.

I drove home wondering about my strange encounter. Once at home, I opened the coin section of my wallet to look at that pink piece of paper. But it wasn't there. I have no idea what happened to it, but it disappeared between the post office and my home.

Was the Guatemalan woman an angel in disguise? I have no idea, but I like to think she was. Even if she wasn't an angel, God was obviously using her. She was no ordinary woman. She knew my secret.

And so did God.

And that comforted me during the divorce and the years after. All I had to do was look at that bracelet and know that God loved me; that He cared what happened to me, that He was with me. Always.

Help Wanted: Divine Domestic

Sandi Banks

IF THERE HAD BEEN AN organization called Moms in Distress, I'd have surely been its poster child that spring day in 1978. My post-partum world had begun unraveling ten days earlier, as I shuffled through the door of our little base house in Woodbridge, England—fresh from the hospital, with a screaming newborn, her energetic fifteen-month-old sister, and an Air Force pilot husband who would soon don his flight suit, fling his large duffel bag into our 1949 Ford Poplar, and wave good-bye as he left on a six-week military deployment. Family and friends were an ocean away. I felt desperately alone.

I'm cheerful by nature, so this was unchartered territory for me: the waves of despair, the heaviness of heart, and the unyielding weight of responsibility.

If I can just make it through this one chore, things will get better, I kept reasoning.

But for every task I completed, three more surfaced. I sank slowly into a recliner that had seen better days and tried to soothe a disgruntled infant and satisfy a needy toddler. Then I surveyed my surroundings and sighed.

Every room looked as if a tsunami had hit. Demands on my time and energy piled up almost as fast as the dirty cloth diapers in the pail. Needs. Everywhere,

needs! Needs of my newborn daughter, whose flailing arms and shrill, round-the-clock cries baffled doctors and unnerved me. Needs of my lively fifteen-month-old, who wandered from room to room, knocking over toy boxes, dumping out hampers, and persistently petitioning Mommy to "weed me a 'tory." Needs, relentless needs, of daily life—the cooking, the cleaning, the toppling mountain of laundry calling my name.

Not just outwardly, but inwardly, a gnawing sense of hopelessness prevailed, as I became physically spent, trying to recover from a difficult delivery and sleepless nights; emotionally drained, missing the moral support of husband, family, and friends; and mentally overwhelmed, spiraling downward without anyone to catch me.

Finally, I just lost it. Loud sobs ushered in a sense of utter despair.

"I give up!" I cried. "Somebody please help me! I can't do this!"

Within moments, over the din of a wailing newborn and babbling toddler, I heard a knock at the door.

"Umm, who's there?" I managed to half-heartedly coax the words out of my mouth, swiping at tears with the back of my hand.

I couldn't imagine who it would be, since surely no one this side of the Atlantic would be paying me a visit. Nor could I imagine anyone seeing my house or me looking like this—the girls and I were far from being in hostess mode. In fact, I wished that whoever it was would just go away. Reluctantly, I navigated through the sea of debris.

Before I could reach the door to unlatch it, it sprung open. A round, rosy-cheeked woman with speckles of gray in her hair and sunshine in her smile invited herself in, latching the door behind her.

"Halloo! Top o' the mornin'!" she chirped, removing her woolly green sweater and multicolored crocheted scarf, carefully draping them over the chair by the door. She put on the tea kettle and made herself quite at home, as if we were long-time girlfriends and I was expecting her visit.

I don't recall her exact words but I do remember the sense of relief I felt when she insisted that I sit and rock the baby, who instantly quieted down and drifted into a blissful sleep—a rare treat for both mother and child.

Before I could gather my wits or utter a word, this stranger started in to work, swiftly and effortlessly, humming as she went.

Her first order of business was to lovingly sweep my sleepy toddler into her arms, kiss her on the cheek, and gently lay her down for a much-needed morning nap. My mother heart melted as my newborn baby snuggled peacefully in my arms, her colicky screams replaced by contented sighs.

Another transformation was taking place around us—at lightning speed. I watched in awe as the mystery woman swiftly tackled the sink full of dishes, the laundry, the sheets, the rugs, the floors—washing, polishing, sweeping, mopping, and even pulling freshly baked meals from the oven. How could a stranger possibly know where everything was, and where everything went—cleaning supplies, pots and pans, clothes, toys—as comfortably as if she lived here herself?

From my little corner of the world, a comfy wooden rocking chair, I watched this amazing metamorphosis unfold.

How surreal! Never could I have imagined such a scene—a stranger taking over my home, and I, totally at peace about it. I don't remember even questioning who she was, where she had come from, or why she was doing this. I just remember an extraordinary calm cascading over me, refreshing and renewing me, as I witnessed my crumbling world returning to order.

In no time at all, I had been given the gift of a sparkling home, sleeping children, scrumptious meals—and peace, "peace that surpasses all understanding."

Then, she was gone. As suddenly as she had come.

"Wait! Please!" I called as she closed the door behind her.

Seconds later I stood on the sidewalk, looking up and down the street. But she was nowhere in sight. I turned to three people who were standing by my house, chatting.

"Which way did she go?"

"Who?"

"The woman who just came out my door!"

They looked at each other, then back at me, and shrugged. They had been there the whole time, yet not one of them had seen anyone enter or leave my house.

Wow. I walked back into my pristine, orderly home, peeked in on my precious babies all snug in their cribs, and marveled, trying to process what had just happened. It would be a while before I could share this story with anyone, or acknowledge what I ultimately came to believe.

God heard my cry and sent an angel to revive my spirit, meet my needs, and above all, to bring Him glory. For they were needs that no one knew about but me. It was a major turning point—not only in my practical need of the moment, but in my spiritual need of a lifetime. I began to realize and confess how far I had drifted from the Lord, not by blatant rebellion, but by busyness and worldly distractions. I could not imagine God loving me that much, listening, caring, providing, in such a dramatic way. It was the first step in my journey back to God's heart.

Who would have thought that a perky woman with a green sweater could play such a critical role in bringing me back to the Lord? It all remains a great mystery. It's unexplainable apart from God's grace and His supernatural response to the plight of a young mom in distress, and her desperate plea for help.

Touched by an Angel

Jennifer Clark Vihel

An open suitcase, partially packed, rested on my bedroom floor. By now, I should have been on a long-awaited trip to London. Instead, I languished in a hospital in a surprise fight for my life.

What I thought was a bad case of food poisoning turned out to be an infected gallbladder. Home alone, I had gone five days without food, hoping that the pain would go away and I'd still make my flight. I had been foolish to wait so long to seek treatment. I now had a gangrenous gallbladder that required emergency surgery.

I woke groggy and in a world of pain. IVs pumped powerful antibiotics and fluids into me, but the infection was bad. My exhaustion felt almost complete, my body's depleted energy storage reminding me of a five-pound bag of sugar with a tear in the bottom. I visualized sugar energy crystals flowing out the hole, only cupfuls remaining before the bag would be completely drained. I wondered what would happen when my energy ran out.

A kind neighbor became my hospital advocate until my family—all currently out of town—could arrive. But with me settled in my room and sleeping, she left to get my daughter from the airport.

That's when I quit breathing.

No bright light called me. Instead, as my breath ebbed away, I felt a seductive pull downward toward a beckoning, black velvet cocoon of a bed. I felt no fear, just an overwhelming longing for the relief and rest that this welcoming bed offered. I had almost reached it when a doctor—who just happened to be walking by— discovered my situation. I came back, surrounded by an excited crew of doctors, nurses, and orderlies. I was whisked away to a different floor where my oxygen level and breathing would be better monitored.

That's when my real battle to survive began. I was weakened from the gangrenous poisons and from the surgery with its nasty, large incision. Now exhausting new yuck—frequent blood draws, IVs that stung, powerful antibiotics that made me ill, a blood transfusion, vomiting, diarrhea, and constant pain—caused me to wonder if the fight was worth it. That velvet bed had seemed so inviting.

I'd always considered myself a fighter, a survivor, and never before this day had I entertained a desire to die. I'd always loved life and embraced it fully. And I had plenty of reasons to want to live. I wanted to see both my girls happy, in love, and with families of their own. I wanted to sell the novel I was currently writing. I wanted to celebrate my upcoming thirtieth wedding anniversary with my husband. But I wasn't afraid to die. And I hurt so much.

Friends and family came. Many prayed for me when I couldn't pray for myself. But when they left for the night, those thoughts of absolute weariness hit hard. I felt utterly spiritless. Recovering seemed enormous. After ten days of this battle, the incredible desire to just stop fighting prowled attractively through my mind.

Weary to the bone, with no more to give, the layers of pain and the depth of this exhaustion overwhelmed me. I wondered if the Lord really had any further purpose for me here. Or was it just my time to go? I longed for God's closeness and I needed to know His will. So I asked God outright: Would it be okay to stop fighting and come home to Him now?

I couldn't sleep that night. My room was dark. A curtain was drawn across the doorway, allowing light from the hallway to filter in below. I waited, expecting the "blood guy" anytime. He usually came around 4:30 for morning draws.

I hated his visits. My veins had become difficult. Multiple pricks had become standard. And his bedside manner was awful. I watched, looking toward the light, dreading his arrival, and hoping today someone different might arrive.

In the highlighted space beneath my curtain, I saw a man's trouser-clad legs and shoes. The man silently entered my darkened room. He was dressed differently, not in the usual hospital garb. Without a word, he moved directly to my bed, reached out, and touched my left shoulder.

Lovely warmth radiated through me. The surging sensation, unlike anything I'd ever felt, flowed throughout my body—offering to me not healing, but an instant reassurance in my dark world of doubt. The warmth lingered after he removed his hand.

I turned, trying to see the man's face. But he had knelt on one knee beside my bed, his head bowed in silent prayer.

His face bathed by shadows, he soon rose and spoke his first words. "God greets you with this new morning and encourages you to embrace it."

My mystery messenger left as quietly as he came, leaving me with the assurance I needed: God wanted me to embrace this new day. It wasn't my time to go.

The "blood guy" entered my room almost on the heels of my anonymous visitor. Wanting to test all other rational possibilities before I dared allow myself to announce my miraculous experience, I mumbled my thanks to him for the prayer. True to form, he scoffed at the idea, and said, "I didn't pray for you."

A pastor perhaps? I briefly thought. But in my heart, I already knew. No matter how many hospital personnel I queried, I knew the truth. That reassuring, radiating touch was not from this world.

God had sent a messenger. I had been touched by an angel.

A second blood transfusion administered later that morning worked wonders. For the first time in ten days, I felt energy flow into me, instead of ebb out. I was still quite ill, but I obediently did my part.

I embraced the new day.

Entertaining Unaware

Maxine Bersch

I SAT BY THE FRONT window cutting out paper dolls and watching the snow pile up across the mountaintop. The flakes had started falling the day before and hadn't let up—an unusually early storm for November in West Virginia. If anything, it was coming down harder now. "Look at the drifts!" I exclaimed. "They've nearly covered the fence." Mother came in from the kitchen. "Looks like it's just going to be us this year," she said. I couldn't help but notice the disappointment in her voice for our Thanksgiving 1928. "No one could get here on a day like this."

I was disappointed too. We lived in the high country, nearly two miles off the main road. Without a telephone, we were pretty isolated, especially come winter. Thanksgiving weather usually made the dirt roads hard with frost, so we could hope for a houseful of guests. After that, we were on our own. I wanted to see my cousins and aunts and uncles as much as Mother did. "We'll have a nice meal to be thankful for," she said, trying to sound cheerful.

Mother always made special dishes: candied sweet potatoes, spiced peaches, cranberries, and crisp celery arranged in a beautiful cut glass dish. My mouth watered just thinking of them. *But wouldn't it taste better if we had guests? I thought.*

Mother went back to the kitchen. Father tended to the fire. I went outside to join my brothers and sisters in a snowball fight.

It wasn't long before we were freezing cold, our clothes soaking wet. The snow was over my boots and melting down into them. Mother beckoned us to come in.

We came in through the back hall, where we hung our coats and hats. Our dog, Major, barking outside, brought us all to the windows that faced the front of the house. "Look!" Mother said. Down by the lower gate, more than one hundred yards from the house, was a man coming quickly through the snow. Dad let Major in the front door, still barking in excitement.

From time to time transients came by in search of a warm meal or a place to spend the night. Mother never turned away anyone. "We might be entertaining angels unaware," she always said.

But that was in the spring and summer, maybe fall. Never in a blizzard! This man didn't even seem bothered by the snow. His long strides never faltered as he walked right to our front door.

"Come in," Dad said. "I'm Seymour Johnson. I don't believe I know you."

"Goodman's the name," the man replied in a cheerful voice. I peered around the corner into the hall for a closer look as Dad helped the man take off his overcoat and hat and ushered him into the sitting room. He was tall like Dad and wore a nice suit. *Strange clothes for a traveler*, I thought. *Didn't he know it was snowing?*

Mother went to welcome him. "He comes from Sandy Low Gap and has to be in Widen tomorrow morning," she reported to us kids in the kitchen, "but the train isn't running today. He set out on foot!"

That town was almost twenty miles north of us. How could he have passed through Sandy Low Gap? The drifts would have been over his head.

"His trousers aren't a bit wet," Mother said. "But never mind that, we have work to do." She didn't have to try to sound cheerful now. We had company for Thanksgiving, even if it was only one stranger. The kitchen became a flurry of activity. Mother asked me to set the table. "Go to the cellar and get a basket of apples," she said. "We need a proper centerpiece for our guest."

We called dinner, and Father brought Mr. Goodman into the dining room, his hand on his shoulder as if they were old friends. We took our seats, and Mother asked our visitor to say grace. I looked at her wide-eyed. She'd never before asked a stranger to pray. But Mr. Goodman didn't even blink before bowing his head. "Dear God," he prayed, "I thank You for the blessings of this day..." His voice was warm and soothing. Mother's "amen" echoed his. We passed the food and waited for him to take the first bite. "Delicious," he said. I had to agree. Thanksgiving dinner had never tasted so good.

"Your father tells me you like horses," Mr. Goodman said to my brother. One by one he engaged all of us in conversation. He listened raptly to stories about horses and schoolwork. He even asked the names of all my dolls. He praised Mother's cooking until she blushed. The apples sparked a lively exchange with Father about horticulture. Mr. Goodman was only one man, but somehow with him at the table the house seemed full of guests. "It's funny," my sister remarked as the dishes were cleared away. "He found a way to turn aside every question we asked about him."

We moved to the sitting room, where Mr. Goodman spied the violin on the bookcase. "Do you play?" he asked Father.

"I saw a bit," Father replied. Soon we were tapping our toes to "Soldier's Joy." Father started clogging. Then Mr. Goodman joined him, to our delight. We ended the evening with popcorn and chestnuts roasted over the fire. I hated to go to bed.

Mother showed our new good friend to his room, and we all said good-night. I could not remember having a better Thanksgiving.

I awoke to the smell of bacon frying. But Mr. Goodman wasn't at the table. "He left sometime during the night," Mother said. "I found this note on the dresser." She read it to all of us kids: "I'll always remember your wonderful family and the hospitality you showed me—the delicious food and after-dinner festivities. May you have many more happy Thanksgiving days. A. Goodman"

Just then Father came in the front door, stamping the snow from his feet. "There are no footprints out there anywhere," Father said.

"Oh my. Do you think—?" Mother paused.

Father nodded, and his voice had a note of joy. "Yes, our visitor was an angel. I'm sure of it."

I've celebrated a lifetime of Thanksgivings since that one, most surrounded by friends and family. But none has ever been more special than the one I spent with A. Goodman. And each year as I reflect on my blessings, I pause to thank God again for answered prayers and the opportunity to entertain unaware.

The Sunshine Girls

Jim Gerron

SCOTCH BURNED MY THROAT ON the way down. *Finally.* I'd waited hours for my favorite bar to open up, and it wasn't even noon yet. I couldn't deny it anymore. My drinking was out of control, and I was scared out of my mind.

"How are things, Jim?" asked Betty the bartender.

I shrugged and looked around the bar. The place was dim—none of the customers wanted to see anything too clearly. I could make out a few faces against the wood paneling: A man in a rumpled coat hunched over a tumbler of whiskey. A woman with dark circles under her eyes. A guy with no teeth sipping a beer. Compared to them I looked great in my designer jeans and expensive haircut, my BMW waiting outside in the rain. But inside I was just as miserable as they were.

I knew I should be happy. I was smart. I was a good salesman. I had my own business selling sunglasses. But none of it made me happy. Once I'd asked a doctor about it. "Don't you have any pills I could take to feel better?" I'd said.

The doctor shook his head. "Pills aren't your answer. You need to find some peace in yourself. Exercise might help. Or meditating. Do you go to church?"

I hadn't been to church in years.

"Sometimes just going into a church can make you feel better. They're good places to think."

I hadn't taken the doctor's advice. Instead I found my own way of lifting my spirits: alcohol. After a few drinks my head was buzzing, and I felt a lot more cheerful. Too bad it couldn't last. As time went on, it took more and more alcohol to make me feel happy. California got hit with a rainy spell, and my business dried up. The worse things got, the more I drank. I told myself I didn't have a problem, that I had it under control.

Then one morning I awoke needing a drink so bad my hands shook and my head ached. I emptied the shot glass in front of me. The alcohol that had once lifted my spirit was now killing it.

"You want another?" asked Betty.

If she only knew how bad.... I pushed myself off the bar stool. "I have to get out of here."

I stepped out into the gray, wet parking lot. The rain pattering on my head was just another reminder of life going wrong. I had to get away—but where? The doctor's words came back to me. *Churches are good places to think.*

I drove out to Manhattan Beach. A steeple rose into the sky up ahead. I parked in front of the church and gazed up at it through the windshield. *Might as well go in*, I thought. *I don't have anywhere else to be.*

I dashed through the rain and ducked inside. The church was empty, but I slipped into the back row of the pews. *Now what?* I wondered. I felt so desperate and alone, I couldn't even appreciate the silence. And then I heard a sound. Way up at the front, to the side of the altar, two little girls were lighting candles. The warm glow of the flames was soothing. I'd forgotten how beautiful votive candles could be.

I don't know what to do, God. I'm scared. I rambled on, watching the candles flicker in the darkness. I told God about my business troubles and my drinking, about the happiness I couldn't find. *I know things have to change, but I don't know how. I just don't want to be miserable anymore. Show me how to be happy, Lord. Show me where to start.*

Up at the altar, the little girls finished lighting their candles. They walked down the aisle together, hand in hand. They looked about the same age. Maybe they were twins. One had long blonde pigtails like spun gold. The other wore her hair loose, but it was the same glorious color. Almost like sunshine. *What are they doing in church at this hour on a school day?* I wondered. They didn't wear school uniforms, but brightly colored dresses like you might see on the beach.

As they passed by my pew the girls turned together and gave me sunny smiles. I nodded to them. *How sweet to be so friendly to a stranger,* I thought. *What must it be like to feel that happy?*

I sat thinking about them. They were the first bright spot in my life since all this rain had started. Maybe even before that.

After a few minutes, I stood up. I'd gotten all I could out of my visit to a church, and it hadn't solved my problems. *So much for that doctor's advice. Time to go face the world.* I ducked my head down and ran to my car, my feet splashing through the puddles. Just as I was about to pull open the car door, something on the windshield caught my eye. I pulled the damp piece of paper out from behind the wiper. It was a note, written in a child's hand. It said: Be happy. God loves you.

I looked at the church, then back to the note. Rain poured onto my head and ran down my collar, but I didn't care. *Be happy. God loves you.*

I scanned the few other cars in the parking lot. None of them had a note on the windshield.

Had the little girls written this? If so, why had they stopped in the rain to write a note? And why did they put a note only on my car? And how had they known which vehicle was mine?

I got into my car, my mind still full of questions. Where would the girls have gotten pencil and paper? They weren't carrying anything when they left the church. In fact, they weren't even wearing raincoats!

What just happened? As if in answer, I felt something change. At first I wasn't sure what. I only knew that I felt different. Something had been lifted from me. I didn't want a drink! The craving I'd lived with for months had vanished. In its place was something new: hope.

The desire for drink never returned. I started attending AA meetings to learn new ways of dealing with my problems. But I was on my way to finding happiness. I knew where to start. With knowing God loved me. I had a sunny note from twin angels to tell me so.

The Night of the Christmas Nurse

Karen Tracy

EMERGENCY MEDICINE DOESN'T TAKE HOLIDAYS off, but this was the first time I'd pulled an EMT shift on Christmas. Already we were racing to a studio apartment in an independent living community to answer the night's first 911 call. I couldn't help thinking this was supposed to be a night of miracles, not injuries.

The ambulance had barely come to a full stop when my partner, Dan, and I jumped out with a gurney. A staff member from the facility waited at the apartment door. "Miss Lily had a fall," she said as we knelt down around the elderly, white-haired woman on the floor. "She's one hundred years old," the staff member informed us with a note of pride.

Miss Lily's studio apartment was neat as a pin. She'd even decorated for the holidays.

"We're going to examine you to see where you're hurt," I told her. Miss Lily nodded. She winced when Dan touched her hip but tried to hide it behind a smile.

"Shortening and rotation of the leg and foot on the affected side," Dan said. Miss Lily winced again. "Increased pain with palpitation to the hip."

Dan and I nodded to each other. It was a classic case of fractured hip—very common in elderly people. We lifted her gingerly onto the gurney, started her IV in the ambulance and headed to the High Desert Medical Center at full speed.

I knew the harsh realities of a broken hip. Many older patients never fully recovered their strength or stopped hurting from their injury. We learned that Miss Lily had been relatively pain-free and strong for one hundred years. Even now she bravely chatted with us between gasps of pain. All that would work in her favor, but it just seemed wrong, somehow, for her to have such a setback on Christmas, of all nights.

Once we got her settled in a hospital bed in the ER, Miss Lily shut her eyes, signaling she was finally overwhelmed by the pain. She looked gray and wilted on the bright white hospital sheets. Colleen, one of the nurses, hooked her up to a cardiac monitor. She pulled the curtain shut around Miss Lily for privacy.

It was Christmas somewhere, but in the ER it looked like any night. Doctors, nurses and EMTs dodged one another to get to patients. I got out of the way and went to the supply closet to restock the ambulance. Afterward I glanced in at Miss Lily. She lay propped up on some pillows, eyes closed, breathing unevenly. *She might not make it through the night*, I thought. It still didn't seem right. Christmas was a time of surprises and miracles, not suffering and death, even after a long life like Miss Lily's.

I sat down outside the ER to catch up on my paperwork before we got another call. When I looked up from my writing I saw Dan pushing the gurney away from Miss Lily's area. I went to help. Just then Colleen popped her head out from behind Miss Lily's curtain. She looked stunned. "What is it?" I asked. ER nurses have seen it all. What was it that had left Colleen speechless?

Instead of answering me, Colleen drew back the curtain. Miss Lily sat there, upright in her bed, beaming.

"Miss Lily," I stammered, "you look much better." Her cheeks were all apples and peaches as she nodded. "Yes, yes," she said. "The medicine worked wonders, just wonders!"

As far as I knew no one had administered any medications to Miss Lily. Colleen confirmed my impression with a shake of her head.

"Which medicine?" I asked.

"Why, the little pill the nurse gave me," she said. "The nice nurse with the white cap."

White cap? Nurses hadn't worn them in decades. My own sister, an RN, had complained about having to wear one for her formal graduation photo. No nurse would bother with a cap while on duty—especially in the ER. And besides, no one would have given Miss Lily any pills. Any medicine would have been administered through the IV in her arm.

But there didn't seem any reason to tell Miss Lily any of that. Instead I just squeezed her hand gently. "Merry Christmas," I said.

Colleen and I stepped around to the other side of the curtain. We faced each other, baffled. "Do you believe in angels?" Colleen whispered.

How else to account for Miss Lily's healing? "Yes," I said. "I do."

I don't know if Miss Lily lived to be 101 or 102 or how old. But I do know that an angel watched over her for the rest of her days. The same angel who brought her comfort that night in the ER. Christmas miracles really can happen anywhere, even when it seems like any other night.

Storybook Ending

Joan Ripley

FINALLY, THE STORM CLOUDS LIFTED! It had rained for nearly two weeks straight, our European vacation better suited for ducks than my two youngest children and me. Still, we'd had a wonderful stay with my elderly cousin, Tante Helga. She'd lived her whole life in Thumersbach, a tiny village of about nine hundred people, and knew the mountains like the back of her hand. A retired obstetrician, she was a friend to everyone in the community. Her villa, on the shore of a lake high up in the Austrian Alps, was like a scene from a storybook. It was magical.

We'd been to cathedrals and museums, castles, outdoor markets, and beautiful gardens, every historical site for miles around. But what I really wanted to do was go hiking.

We'd come all this way, from our home an hour outside of New York City to walk the Alps. I wanted Mark, ten, and Sandy, seven, to see my birthplace in all its rugged, breathtaking, snow-capped glory, to run through alpine meadows and dip their feet in ice-cold streams. But in the mountains storms can quickly turn deadly. No adventure was worth putting the kids in danger.

So that morning, when the sun burst over the horizon, it was like a gift from God. Right after breakfast, my friend Wolfgang knocked on the door. "C'mon, what are we waiting for?" he said. "It's a perfect day to touch the sky."

"Really?" Sandy said, her eyes wide with wonder. This was the moment—the magic—I'd been waiting for.

"We'll take the chairlift up," Wolfgang said. "Then have a picnic at the top and a leisurely hike back down." His wife and two children would come too. I could already see us dancing through a field of wildflowers, just like the von Trapps.

"I can't wait to hear all about it," Tante Helga said. We hugged her good-bye and set off on our excursion. The chairlift swayed gently, carrying us over the treetops, higher and higher, above the timberline. "Look," I said to Sandy beside me. Below us blue gentians and alpine laurel bloomed among the rocks. Above us, almost close enough to touch, was a powder-blue sky, and in the distance snow-capped peaks stood guard.

"Cool," said Sandy. I agreed.

Near the summit we feasted on a lunch of black bread, cheese, and cold cuts, then drank our fill from a clear, pure mountain spring. The boys chased after each other, while the girls picked bouquets of wildflowers. Far below us birds circled lazily over the valley. In a meadow we spied some brown cows, their eyes large and gentle, their colorful bells serenading us as they grazed. No one seemed to be watching them but I knew that milk cows were often let loose on the high alpine pastures where they could eat their fill of meadow grasses.

"High on a hill was a lonely goatherd," I sang out.

"*Lay ee odl lay ee odl lay hee hoo,*" the kids answered.

I looked to Wolfgang to join in, but he was staring at the sky. "A storm's moving in," he said. "We need to find the trail and head down."

I glanced upward. Black clouds blotted out the sun. In the distance we heard the rumble of thunder. "Let's hurry," I said.

We quickly reached the trailhead, Wolfgang in the lead, his long legs stretching farther with every step. Fat raindrops splattered on my arms.

We reached the forest, hoping for safety, but under the canopy it was nearly as dark as night, broken only by jagged flashes of lightning above our heads. We could barely find our way. Wind lashed the treetops, branches bent and swayed madly. The rain fell in sheets, pelting us as we zigzagged down the switchback. My feet stumbled against rocks, yet there was no choice but to press on. Every minute we were outside increased the danger of a lightning strike. "I'm scared," Sandy cried. "My feet can't go this fast."

"I'll carry you," Wolfgang shouted above the din. He lifted her, holding her tight against his waist. "But we need to go faster. The storm's getting worse. Our best chance is to go straight down—to the road at the bottom. Follow me."

With Sandy in his arms, he turned and crashed through the undergrowth. We scrambled after him. I struggled to keep my balance. Branches clawed at our arms and faces. My hair and clothes were drenched. Water streamed down my back. I felt helpless. A flash of lightning, followed immediately by a deafening thunderclap exploding in the nearby trees made us realize that the storm was now directly overhead. Trembling with fear, I grabbed a branch to steady myself. "Angel of God," I pleaded, "please protect us." Could God even hear my pleas over the storm? Heaven had never seemed farther away. I stumbled after Wolfgang and the others. The trees seemed to be thinning. I stepped into a clearing, though the rain was falling so hard it was difficult to see more than a few yards in front of me.

"Look," Mark said. "I see a light. There must be a house."

I saw it too. I could just barely make out a cottage. "Let's run for it," I said. I took Mark's hand, our feet slipping and sliding on the grass.

What if no one's home? But just before Wolfgang reached it, the door swung open. As if we were expected.

An old man wearing the faded lumber jacket of a woodcutter stood inside the doorway. "*Grüss Gott,*" he greeted us, a gracious smile spreading across his face. He motioned us to a fire that filled every corner of the room with a golden glow. There he handed each of us a blanket and helped us spread our soggy clothes on the hearth. The fire's radiance and the old man's kindness made the room more than warm and cozy. The Austrians have a word for it: *gemütlich*. And that's exactly what the cottage felt like—*gemütlich*. In a heavenly sort of way.

I soaked up the warmth of the blaze, barely noticing that our host had stepped away. He returned carrying a tray with a plate of cookies and mugs of piping hot chocolate, topped with puffs of whipped cream. "This will make you feel better," he said.

"*Mmmmmmmm*," said the kids, licking the cream from their lips. It was delicious. But puzzling. Would he have made all this for himself or was he expecting company? "Thank you," Wolfgang said. "I don't know how much farther we could have made it. I feel bad. I should have been watching the weather more closely."

"No need to explain," the old woodcutter said. "I know exactly what happened. You were having fun."

His voice was gentle and soothing, almost like music. The stress of the storm had melted away. I felt completely at ease, as if we were spending the afternoon with a dear friend. We barely noticed that the rain had ended and the thunder had wandered off, grumbling to itself.

I looked out the window. The late afternoon sun shone brightly through the curtains. Tante Helga! She'd be worried about us if we were late. "Your clothes are dry," our host said, as if he'd read my mind. "You'll be fine going home. Just follow the path to the bridge, then turn left and it will take you to a road that goes right past your aunt's house."

Perfect. We said our good-byes and set off down the trail. It wasn't until we reached the bridge that I wondered: How had he known where we were staying? *Tante Helga knows everyone around here*, I reminded myself. *She must have told him about us.* I turned around for one last wave but saw no one. No house. Not

even the clearing. The trees are probably blocking my view, I thought. But I hadn't even noticed that we were back in the forest.

We found the road and soon were back at Tante Helga's, just like the woodcutter had said. "You're totally dry," she said. "How did you miss the storm?"

We told her about the house in the woods. Her face grew more puzzled with every word.

"I know the cottage you're talking about," she said, "but it burned down fifty years ago."

"But the old woodcutter," Sandy said. "Was he a ghost?"

Tante Helga shook her head. "*Nein*," she said. "Not a ghost. An angel. Sent to watch over you."

I thought of the prayer I'd said, lost in the crashing of the thunder. God had heard every word. He'd given us shelter even in the midst of the storm.

The Host of Heaven

Dr. S. Ralph Harlow

IT WAS NOT CHRISTMAS; IT was not even wintertime, when the event occurred that for me threw sudden new light on the ancient angel tale.

It was a glorious spring morning and we were walking, my wife and I, through the newly budded birches and maples near Ballardvale, Massachusetts.

Now I realize that this, like any account of personal experience, is only as valid as the good sense and honesty of the person relating it. What can I say about myself? That I am a scholar who shuns guesswork and admires scientific investigation? That I have an AB from Harvard, an MA from Columbia, a PhD from Hartford Theological Seminary? That I have never been subject to hallucinations? That attorneys have solicited my testimony, and I have testified in the courts, regarded by judge and jury as a faithful, reliable witness? All this is true and yet I doubt that any amount of such credentials can influence the belief or disbelief of another.

In the long run, each of us must sift what comes to us from others through his own life experience, his view of the universe, his understanding. And so I will simply tell my story.

The little path on which Marion and I walked that morning was spongy to our steps and we held hands with the sheer delight of life as we strolled near a lovely brook. It was May, and because it was the examination reading period for students at Smith College where I was a professor, we were able to get away for a few days to visit Marion's parents.

We frequently took walks in the country, and we especially loved the spring after a hard New England winter, for it is then that the fields and the woods are radiant and calm yet show new life bursting from the earth. This day we were especially happy and peaceful; we chatted sporadically, with great gaps of satisfying silence between our sentences.

Then from behind us we heard the murmur of muted voices in the distance, and I said to Marion, "We have company in the woods this morning."

Marion nodded and turned to look. We saw nothing, but the voices were coming nearer—at a faster pace than we were walking, and we knew that the strangers would soon overtake us. Then we perceived that the sounds were not only behind us but also above us, and we looked up.

How can I describe what we felt? Is it possible to tell of the surge of exaltation that ran through us? Is it possible to record this phenomenon with objective accuracy and yet be credible?

For about ten feet above us, and slightly to our left, was a floating group of glorious, beautiful creatures that glowed with spiritual beauty. We stopped and stared as they passed above us.

There were six of them, young beautiful women dressed in flowing white garments and engaged in earnest conversation. If they were aware of our existence they gave no indication of it. Their faces were perfectly clear to us, and one woman, slightly older than the rest, was especially beautiful. Her dark hair was pulled back in what today we would call a ponytail, and although I cannot say it was bound at the back of her head, it appeared to be. She was talking intently to a younger spirit whose back was toward us and who looked up into the face of the woman who was talking.

Neither Marion nor I could understand their words although their voices were clearly heard. The sound was somewhat like hearing but being unable to understand a group of people talking outside a house with all the windows and doors shut.

They seemed to float past us, and their graceful motion seemed natural—as gentle and peaceful as the morning itself. As they passed, their conversation grew fainter and fainter until it faded out entirely, and we stood transfixed on the spot, still holding hands and still with the vision before our eyes.

It would be an understatement to say that we were astounded. Then we looked at each other, each wondering if the other also had seen.

There was a fallen birch tree just there beside the path. We sat down on it and I said, "Marion, what did you see? Tell me exactly, in precise detail. And tell me what you heard."

She knew my intent—to test my own eyes and ears; to see if I had been the victim of hallucination or imagination. And her reply was identical in every respect to what my own senses had reported to me.

I have related this story with the same faithfulness and respect for truth and accuracy as I would tell it on the witness stand. But even as I record it I know how incredible it sounds.

Perhaps I can claim no more for it than that it has had a deep effect on our own lives. For this experience of almost thirty years ago greatly altered our thinking. Once both Marion and I were somewhat skeptical about the absolute accuracy of the details at the birth of Christ. The story, as recorded by St. Luke, tells of an angel appearing to shepherds abiding in the field and after the shepherds had been told of the Birth, "suddenly there was with the angel a multitude of the heavenly host praising God, and saying, Glory to God in the highest" (Luke 2:8-14, KJV).

As a child I accepted the multitude seen by the shepherds as literal heavenly personages. Then I went through a period when I felt that they were merely symbols injected into a fantasy or legend. Today, after the experience at Ballardvale, Marion and I are no longer skeptical. We believe that in back of that story recorded by St. Luke lies a genuine objective experience told in wonder by those who had the experience.

Once, too, we puzzled greatly over the Christian insistence that we have "bodies" other than our normal flesh and blood ones. We were like the doubter of whom St. Paul wrote: "But some man will say, How are the dead raised up? and with what body do they come?" (I Corinthians 15:35, KJV).

In the thirty years since that bright May morning, His answer has rung for us with joyous conviction.

"There are also celestial bodies, and bodies terrestrial: but the glory of the celestial is one, and the glory of the terrestrial is another...So also is the resurrection of the dead...It is sown a natural body; it is raised a spiritual body. There is a natural body, and there is a spiritual body...And as we have borne the image of the earthy, we shall also bear the image of the heavenly...For this corruptible must put on incorruption, and this mortal must put on immortality" (I Corinthians 15:40–53, KJV).

All of us, I think, hear the angels for a little while at Christmastime. We let the heavenly host come close once in the year. But we reject the very possibility that what the shepherds saw two thousand years ago was part of the reality that presses close every day of our lives.

And yet there is no reason for us to shrink from this knowledge. Since Marion and I began to be aware of the host of heaven all about us, our lives have been filled with a wonderful hope.

The experience at Ballardvale, added to the convictions of my Christian faith, gives me not only a feeling of assurance about the future, but a sense of adventure toward it too.

The Lady with Red Hair

Morna Gilbert

HER PIERCING GREEN EYES AND vibrant red hair did not belong in the sterile gray hospital room permeated with breathing machine sounds, a beeping monitor, and the air of gloom. Only my crushed body matched my depressed emotions. Strapped to tubes and traction, unable to go anywhere and knowing they were lying to me about the condition of my new bride, I was sure hopelessness would become my new norm.

The seventy-mile-an-hour head-on collision—caused by a drunk driver—had left my wife and me in pieces. I would survive, but be crippled the rest of my life. My bride? Who knows? I longed to hold her and tell her everything would be fine but I couldn't even visit her—let alone comfort her.

"The Lord is my shepherd..." the soft comforting voice read.

Who is this red-headed lady? I wondered as I glanced through the side bars of my bed.

"I shall not want..." She continued reading into the wee hours of the night.

Like the regular ticking of a clock, the nurse with red hair came to my room night after night and read the Psalms—then the Gospels—as I would rudely drift off into a deep sleep. I became dependent on her timing, her comforting, her embracing, her encouraging. As I physically healed I knew the nurse with red

hair had a big part in my emotional healing also. Though we never carried on a conversation—my heart longed to thank her.

Many weeks passed as I was in and out of surgeries, therapy, and grueling hospital routines. My bride was far worse off than I was, but she was alive. The hospital staff managed to push me in a wheelchair to visit her once in a great while. I told her of the sweet nurse with red hair who visited me on a nightly basis. I wished she had time to visit my wife—the comforting words would have given her the same healing they had brought me. Oh, the faithfulness of that lady with red hair.

Once I became more mobile I was moved to another floor of the hospital—where the nurse with the red hair was unable to visit me. One day I asked permission from the hospital staff to visit the red-haired, green-eyed nurse. Escorted in a wheelchair I went directly to the nurse's station and asked for the senior nurse. With a firm resolve I asked to see the nurse with red hair. I told her how faithful she had been and I wanted to personally thank her. I told of her consistency in reading the Scriptures to me and how life-giving and encouraging those words had been. My emotions let loose with tears as I shared with the senior nurse how my heart had been healed of all anger and bitterness toward the drunk driver who had caused all this pain in my wife's and my life—because of the lady with red hair. As my passionate plea grew, the nurse quieted me down and slowly shared these words: "I'm sorry, sir. We have no nurses here with red hair."

Angels of Mount Ypsilon

Heather LeMasurier

THE SKY WAS BLUE, THE sun was warm. A perfect summer day for hiking. Atop 13,507-foot Mount Ypsilon, where my husband, Wes, and I had just eaten a packed lunch of sandwiches, apples and fruitcake, the view extended for mile after glorious mile of snowcapped Rocky Mountain peaks. It was Friday, the day Wes and I hiked together each week. Mount Ypsilon was one of our favorite routes. We'd climbed it at least three times in the forty-one years we'd lived in Colorado, where Wes had taught geology at the University of Colorado and I'd worked as a nurse. Now we were retired with grown kids and schedules blissfully free for getting outdoors. We spent as much time in the mountains as possible. We felt at home there. Close to God and the angels. Safe.

Which probably explains why, when Wes stopped to take a photo, I didn't wait for him but instead kept right on descending the gray, rocky talus below the summit. There was no trail, just occasional cairns of stones marking the way to where the tundra began. It was chilly and windy up there, still dotted with remnants of winter snow. I shouted back to Wes that I was turning off the ridgeline toward the trail. I wasn't sure of the exact way we'd come up—I always let Wes the geologist do our map-reading—but I figured I'd hit the trail eventually. There aren't too many ways you can go from a summit but down. Besides, I usually walked ahead of Wes

on descents. A bad knee slowed him downhill. I'd wait for him once I reached the trail.

I clattered down, clicking on rocks with my trekking poles. The wind pushed and pulled. Suddenly I stopped. Before me a steep cliff dropped away, plunging hundreds of feet. Huh? We hadn't passed any cliffs coming up. I turned around to show Wes. But I couldn't make him out. A wall of talus rose behind me. The wind blew against my face.

Figuring I'd taken a wrong turn, I climbed back to where I thought I'd left Wes. He wasn't there. I took off in a new direction. Moments later I stood atop the same cliff. I shaded my eyes with my hand. Everywhere the view was the same. Featureless gray rock, peaks ringing the horizon. I assured myself I wasn't lost.

I retraced my steps twice more. The fourth time I found myself at the cliff I admitted the obvious. I was lost. I took my water bottle from my pack. It was empty. Wes and I had drained it that morning like we always do, lightening my load first. A twinge of nervousness seized me. The sun was halfway to the horizon. Where was Wes? No doubt he'd figured I was way ahead as usual. How long until he realized I wasn't on the trail? The trailhead was five miles down. Wes wouldn't reach the car until late afternoon.

I looked around. The sun was warm but I knew the minute it set, the temperature would plunge. Like always I had a wool hat, gloves, fleece, rain parka, poncho and a down sweater in my pack, along with a first aid kit and plenty of nuts and raisins for snacking. *Would that be enough for a night below freezing?*

Keep calm, Heather. Just that morning Wes and I had listened to a news segment on the radio about lost hikers. Stay put, experts recommend, so rescuers can find you. Okay, I'd stay put. Maybe Wes would reach the trailhead in time to alert rangers and they'd have someone up here before nightfall.

Nightfall. The word loomed in my mind. I needed to do something to keep busy. I began stacking rocks into an improvised shelter. Already the wind was finding its way into my parka. An hour later I had a small circle of raised stones.

I sat in it. The wind howled around me. I stared at the landscape. Suddenly the mountains I so loved seemed altogether different. I was seized with fear. I did not want to sleep on this peak.

In desperation I cried out, *God! Help me! I need an angel!*

With a sudden burst of energy I picked myself up, stuffed my water bottle with snow and set off along the slope, determined to find that trail. I ranged this way and that, always keeping my little shelter in view. Suddenly my heart leapt. There, over a rise, I saw a tiny pile of rock. A cairn! A trail marker. "Thank you, God!" I cried. From the cairn I could see another cairn. And another. It was definitely the trail. I picked up the pace, glancing at the sky. Could I make it down before dark? Never had I hiked so fast.

My spirits soon fell. The cairns ended at the beginning of grassy tundra. I saw no trail. It was too early in the year. Not enough people had hiked up here to flatten the grass. Wes must have navigated by map. Was I lost again?

I stared down the slope toward a saddle between two peaks. To my immense relief a man stood in the middle of the saddle. He wore dark clothes. I waved my trekking poles and shouted but he didn't seem to notice me. Staring at him I realized he was standing directly on the trail. I hadn't seen it before but now I discerned it continuing down the slope behind him. I hurried down, watching my footing. I reached the saddle. The man was gone.

I continued along the trail, thinking I might see the man. Instead, a few miles down, I came to a crossroads. Which way had Wes and I come? Surely I was near the trailhead. *Just pick the right trail, Heather....* I set off down one that looked right. It plunged into a thick wood. The setting sun barely illuminated the trees.

I was just beginning to lose sight of the trail when it ended at a damp marsh. The sun was gone. With a sinking feeling I knew I was not going to make it home that day. I was going to have to spend the night outside. Wearily I hiked away from the marsh until I couldn't see a thing. I lay between two downed trees surrounded by close, damp woods. I ate some nuts, drank my melted snow water,

took two Advil and prayed. The wood became utterly silent. In the dark I felt a wonderful sensation—someone cradling me, dispelling all fear. I fell asleep and awoke to the sound of birds. I hastened back up the trail.

I'd barely reached the crossroads when I saw a man walking quickly uphill. My heart flooded with relief. That must be the way down. Oddly, the man was wearing nothing but shorts and a T-shirt. It was cold! I asked if he'd come up from his car. He said yes and continued on without another word. Eager to get home I hurried down myself. Not ten minutes later I came to the end of the trail and heard a shout. A ranger clambered out of a pickup saying she'd been praying for me all night. I practically collapsed from joy.

The ranger told me Wes had come down the trail late the previous afternoon and reported me missing. Rescuers had sent him home to Boulder to e-mail photos of me. What an awful night he must have had! He was on his way back now, the ranger said. Had I been gone another fifteen minutes they'd have sent helicopters to look for me.

The ranger said one more thing. When I told her how grateful I was for the man I'd seen on the trail that morning, she gave me a funny look and said no one had been up that trail since she'd come on duty at 3:00 AM. All those hours I'd felt so lost and alone on that vast, beautiful mountain—I wasn't lost at all. I was right at home. I was close to God and the angels. I was safe.

The Vision

Karen Hall

IT WAS JUST A RINGING telephone, but it filled me with dread. As I reached out to answer it, I remembered the phone call I'd received only weeks before. The phone call from the hospital telling me my daughter, Ashley, had been in a terrible car accident. Whatever this call was about, it couldn't hurt me. The worst had already happened. Ashley was dead.

Back in my kitchen, I lifted the phone off the hook. "Hi, Karen, it's Kim. Something just happened down at Roy's Market."

Kim was a good friend of mine. Roy's Market was the store down the road, the one that sat beside the cemetery where we'd buried Ashley. I barely followed what Kim was saying. I could barely follow anything these days. I had a husband to take care of, and two younger children. Now I also had Skyler, Ashley's baby, who, at only six weeks old, had survived the accident. Everyone said it was a miracle, and I knew I should be grateful. But I couldn't think about anything but Ashley. She'd been taken so young. I tried to picture her in heaven. How could I be sure she made it there safely? *God, I need to know she's with You.*

Kim was still talking. I forced myself to make sense of her words. A woman had come into Roy's Market—a stranger. She heard everyone talking about Ashley and was moved beyond words. She wanted to pay for the tombstone. "Just take her phone number," Kim said gently. "You can call her anytime."

I wrote down the number and hung up. I didn't want anyone paying for my daughter's tombstone. I'd already put a down payment on it. I wasn't sure how I would pay the balance when the stone was finished. For now I just had to struggle through the day. It was all I could do to get dressed.

My sister-in-law, Becky, came by to help with the housework. When I told her about the call from Roy's Market, she decided to check it out. "What would make a complete stranger offer such a kindness?" she wanted to know. While Becky talked on the phone, I dwelled on my worries. *God, where is Ashley? Is she safe?*

I don't know how long Becky spoke to the woman on the phone. Tears streamed down her face.

"Did the woman know Ashley?" I asked when she hung up.

Becky shook her head and told me the story. "Driving past the cemetery, the woman noticed fresh flowers on a new grave. A group of people filed up to it. At least she thought they were people. As she got closer she saw . . ."

Becky paused. "What?" I said.

"Angels. A community of angels surrounded the grave."

The woman had to stop the car to pray. Even though she had no idea whose grave it was. Afterward she stopped in Roy's Market. The folks there were talking about Ashley's accident. The woman asked where she was buried and to describe the exact spot in the cemetery. It was the grave the angels had visited.

For the first time since her death I cried tears of relief. Ashley was in heaven with God and His angels. If she couldn't be in my arms, at least she could be in His. I could hold tight to my grandson, grateful that I still had a piece of Ashley with me on earth.

The tombstone was finished weeks later. The balance had been paid anonymously. But Becky and I knew who was responsible. She dug out the number and called to thank her, but the number no longer worked.

I didn't need a phone number to thank God for her. One of Ashley's angels, sent to bring me comfort.

CHAPTER 3

Glimpses of Heaven

Flock of Angels

R. T. Brown

IN AND OUT OF THE hospital—that's where I was that winter I was seventy-three. My wife, Mary, and I had barely been able to enjoy our usual respite in south Florida. I couldn't help thinking my thirty years of heart problems had finally caught up to me.

I believed in God and heaven, but still I wondered: What would happen to me when I died? The thought terrified me. I didn't want to leave my wife and family. I didn't ever want to be without them. Especially without knowing what awaited me. Then I had an experience I'll never forget. It began with emergency surgery. In the ICU recovering, I drifted in and out of consciousness.

"His heart! It's stopped beating."

"Code blue!"

Pounding on my chest, doctors shouted orders. Nurses darted here and there. Amid the flurry of activity, I felt myself rising, rising right off the bed and up to the ceiling. I looked down and saw my body lying in the bed. A doctor put paddles to my chest. A cold sensation. A noise. My body jumped from the charge, but I felt nothing.

"He's dead. We've lost him."

I'm dead. I'm really dead. All my fears realized. Where do I go now?

I floated through the wall like it was not even there and found myself in a brightly lit tunnel that seemed to have no end. *What am I doing here? Where am I going?* My thoughts stopped. I hurtled through the tunnel—my body sucked through it as if by some powerful vacuum. Large white flakes—like snow but not cold—filled the air. I became frightened. *Wherever I'm headed is farther and farther away from my wife. How to get back? Or can't I?*

The tunnel opened into a vast space. Not a second to catch my breath, I shot straight up…through layers of thick clouds.

I floated. Far, far below me were the clouds I'd passed through, stretching across the horizon. I was completely alone, helpless, in some mysterious distant cosmos. *Dear God, please show me comfort.*

Far in the distance I saw movement. It was coming toward me, effortlessly gliding through the air. A flock, of some sort. The creatures had wings, huge feathered appendages the size of their bodies. Birds? I glanced nervously around.

But there was nowhere to go. The creatures were within one hundred feet.

Then I saw.

Angels.

One of them broke away from the group. I could almost touch him. I couldn't make out his face and yet, there was something familiar about him. "I know you. You're my guardian angel."

The angel didn't say a word. His robes rustled, and his face passed gently against my cheek. Like a kiss.

My worries vanished. I felt a peace I had never known. All was quiet. And in the stillness God was there, welcoming me, enveloping me in His love.

I looked over the angel's shoulder to the horizon beyond. "Lord, by Your grace," I said, "I'm ready to come home with You."

A voice, soothing yet powerful responded: "It's not your time yet. You must go back."

A force pulled me back exactly the way I came, even faster this time. I plummeted straight down, almost in free fall, plunging, plunging through the clouds.

Something's wrong! I'm going to crash! Help me!

I stopped falling and smoothly turned in to the tunnel, still filled with white flakes. I flew to the end, back through the hospital walls. I saw my body—still in the bed—doctors and nurses crowded around.

"His heart's beating. He's alive!"

I'm alive. I'm back on the earth. Everything went dark.

It was sometime later when I felt myself stirring. I opened my eyes, and there was Mary. "I thought we'd lost you," she said.

I looked into her eyes. "I went to the most wonderful place," I said and told her my story.

It's been three years since I was granted that glimpse into the Hereafter. In a few weeks Mary and I will pack up and head north to greet the spring. I can't wait to see our children and grandkids. Someday I know my time here will end. But I'm not worried. I know where I'm going, and that God will be there to welcome me home.

"An Angel Picked Me Up and We Flew"

by James L. Garlow & Keith Wall

THE BUETTNER FAMILY—CRAIG AND Amy and their five small children—had just one thing on their minds: baseball. Little League baseball, to be exact. The oldest of the kids, ten-year-old Jacob, was a member of the top-seeded team in that year's championship series. Craig, a Tuscaloosa family physician and the University of Alabama football team doctor, was serving as assistant coach. As they prepared for the first game that afternoon, expectations were high. The adults decided to give the boys extra incentive by promising to throw a swim party after the game.

Forty people, most of them children, crowded into the backyard of one of the team families that evening. One dad grilled hot dogs and hamburgers while the rest of the parents supervised the kids in the pool. When it was time for dinner, everyone was herded out of the water and into the yard, where they sat on towels and blankets. Craig settled his kids down with plates of food. Four-year-old Kennedy, in his baggy red swimsuit, sat on a nearby towel with other children. Amy focused her attention on their five-week-old baby, Mark. Craig brought Amy a hamburger and finally sat down himself to enjoy a few moments' relaxation before the party moved back to the pool.

"I took one bite and felt like God gently tapped me on the shoulder and told me to find Kennedy," Amy recalled. "Somehow I knew before I ever turned around and looked that he was not on that towel with his brother anymore." She ran to search the yard.

Then Craig experienced the kind of horrific moment that haunts a parent's nightmares. He heard Jacob screaming, and ran to find him: "Daddy, Daddy, we found Kennedy! He was at the bottom of the pool!"

When he arrived, he was surprised to see his son lying on the concrete at the pool's edge. Jacob and two other young boys had already dived in and retrieved him from beneath nine feet of water in the deep end. Kennedy was out of the pool—but the sight of him added to Craig's growing alarm. The boy's body was deep blue. His skin was bloated and his belly looked like he was "nine months pregnant." Craig immediately began to administer CPR. Between five and ten minutes later, the boy began to thrash around and exhibit behavior that doctors call "abnormal posturing," a kind of muscle seizure that indicates severe brain damage—and usually precedes death. At eleven minutes, paramedics arrived.

Several hours later, Craig and Amy arrived at the intensive care unit of Children's Hospital in Birmingham, Alabama. While Kennedy had been transported from Tuscaloosa in a helicopter, they traveled the fifty miles by car—a trip that seemed to take, Craig said, "about five years." Kennedy was now on a ventilator and attached to an array of IVs and instruments. He was restrained and paralyzed with drugs to keep him from thrashing around in the bed and further injuring himself.

The doctor in charge did not sugarcoat the assessment he gave the Buettners that night. Based on clinical measurements of Kennedy's condition, he estimated the boy had only a fifteen percent chance of survival. If he lived, there was only a one percent chance he'd recover to lead a normal life.

For Amy, the next forty-eight hours were a blur: meetings with doctors; nursing the baby, Mark; and fighting desperately to hang on to hope. On the third day, Amy was alone in the room with Kennedy, her Bible open on the bed. She asked

God what she should read, and the answer came to her: "Psalm 18." As she read, one verse leapt from the page as if it were lit up in neon: "He reached down from on high and took hold of me; he drew me out of deep waters.... He brought me out into a spacious place; he rescued me because he delighted in me."

"It was like a switch turned on," she said, "and I just knew that God was going to draw Kennedy out of 'deep waters' and rescue him."

Later that day, doctors took Kennedy off the medication keeping him immobile. The next day, doctors reluctantly took him off the ventilator. He coughed and sputtered as the tube came out of his throat. Amy held him in her arms for the first time. She could finally ask him the question that had haunted her for five days: "Baby, what happened?"

His answer was not what she expected to hear. "I was in a whirlpool, then an angel picked me up, and we flew," he said, in his quiet, gravelly voice. "We flew through walls, and I flew through you, Mommy."

One week after arriving at the hospital with a ninety-nine percent chance of being paralyzed and severely impaired cognitively for the rest of his life—Kennedy Buettner went home.

Over the next few days, Kennedy talked more about things he had experienced after he went into the water. The following conversation is compressed, having taken place over several days: When the angel picked you up, where did you go? I went to heaven. What did you see? I saw Jesus. I saw lots of people and angels. They were very happy. I saw a door with jewels on it. There was snow on the other side when they opened it.

Amy takes comfort from the fact that, even in the grip of a potentially frightening death, Kennedy didn't suffer and wasn't afraid. "There was no sting of death for him," she said. "All Kennedy remembers was he was in a whirlpool—which might have been the sensation of water swirling around him—and an angel picked him up. There was no struggle and no pain. He went straight to heaven."

The Stranger

by Renee Coy

I WAS CLEARING UP THE breakfast dishes when the phone rang. "Something's happened to your mom," my dad said. He was trying to keep calm, but I could hear panic in his voice. "The ambulance should be here any minute."

A rush of cold swept through my body, as if I could feel the blood draining to my feet. "Ambulance?"

"I found her collapsed on the floor. Hurry over! I'm alone here."

I stumbled upstairs, jerked on my shoes, and ran out to the car. Luckily my family lived close together. My parents were only a few minutes away. I pulled out of my driveway and sped down the two-lane highway.

Mom hasn't been well since the accident, I thought as I drove. She'd been hit by lightning and hadn't truly recovered. *God, be with her!*

The front door to the house was thrown open when I arrived. I found my dad performing CPR in the hallway. Mom was stretched out on the floor in front of him. He looked up at me as I entered, his eyes full of anguish, his face white to the lips, sweaty with fear. I knew I'd carry the picture of it in my mind forever.

"Hang on, Mom," I said, dropping to my knees to help Dad with the compressions. One, two, three...I counted them as I'd been taught in a life-saving course

I'd taken at school. But would CPR be enough to help Mom? I touched my fingers to her wrist. No pulse. "Dear God, help us!" I said. "Help her, God!"

I leaned out the front door to search for the ambulance. The two-lane highway stretched out in both directions. Empty. About a hundred yards west, a gravel road turned off it toward a creek and picnic area. All quiet. Not a soul to be seen. How long since Dad had called for help? I wondered. *When will they get here?* "God, we need you!" I said. I started to turn from the doorway. Out of the corner of my eye I saw a flurry of movement across the road. Suddenly there was a man there. Alone. *Where did he come from?* Not a second before the road had been empty.

The man took slow steps one way, then turned on his heels and walked in the other direction. He held his hands clasped behind his back, his head hung low as if in serious contemplation, and he paced. Back and forth, slowly and with determination. Why was this stranger pacing in front of our house? I knew everyone in our small community. I'd never seen this man in my life.

"It's no use!" Dad said. The man was still visible through the open door. He looked agitated, as if waiting for something. "I hear the ambulance!" I said.

The white vehicle pulled up with its whirling lights and screeching tires, and a team of EMTs jumped out.

"We need oxygen! She's not breathing!" I called to them.

Dad and I got out of their way. All I could do now was pray. I bowed my head and prayed harder than I ever had before. When I opened my eyes I was looking at the man again. He was still pacing back and forth, his hands clasped behind him, his head bent. His loose, soft-gray tunic came down to his knees over loose brown trousers. I could see even from a distance that his outfit was made of linen. The intricate weave of the material seemed to shine in the early morning light. On his feet were braided leather sandals. Even in the chaos of the moment the man looked out of place. This was a farming community. Men wore Levi's or overalls with plaid or denim shirts. On another day I might have puzzled over where the man could have come from, but this wasn't another day. The wall clock ticked away the minutes as the EMTs gave Mom oxygen. There was no change. One of them took her pulse again. He looked up at me and shook his head. "She's gone."

I covered my face and wept.

The EMTs took Mom into the ambulance. Two of my aunts and uncles happened by and comforted Dad as best they could. I walked out to the road as the ambulance pulled away. How can this be happening? I thought as the taillights disappeared around a bend in the road. It didn't seem real. I had prayed for God's presence here. But Mom was gone.

My Aunt Leila came up beside me and gave me a squeeze. I barely felt it. She started to lead me back into the house and then paused. "Who is that man?" she asked, nodding across the road.

He had stopped his frantic pacing. Now he was walking right up to me. Although his expression was calm and soothing, the air around him almost seemed to crackle with energy. His clothing glowed with the strange sheen I'd noticed earlier. His eyes were large and dark. His voice, when he spoke, was low and smooth. "I am sorry about your mother," he said, looking into my eyes.

Before I could reply, he went back across the street. He hadn't bothered to check for traffic.

"Who is that?" Aunt Leila asked again. "How do you know him?"

"I don't." So how had he known it was my mother who had just died?

We went inside, where the rest of the family was watching. No one had seen the man before and between all of us we knew everyone in the vicinity. I lingered in the doorway to see where the stranger would go. He returned to the spot where he had been pacing. Then he was gone.

I stepped out into the yard and looked up and down the highway, and down the gravel road. There was no sign of him. One second he was there, and in the next second he was gone. As if he had vanished right before my eyes.

Everything about this stranger was adding up to something incredible. This was no man.

That night in bed I went over every detail of what I'd seen, from the flutter that had announced the stranger's presence to the kindness in his eyes. I knew he was not a man. Nor was he a healing angel sent to save Mom's life, or a warrior angel like I'd read about in the Bible. This was a different kind of angel. An angel who waited to escort Mom to her new home in heaven.

Angels All Around

by James L. Garlow & Keith Wall

IT WAS HARD TO BELIEVE that one week earlier Ryan was at home with his younger brother, Jordan, watching cartoons and eating Popsicles while the two boys recovered from routine cases of chicken pox.

When one large pock behind Ryan's ear turned red and began to swell, Cheryl and her husband, Jeff, weren't too worried. But as the swelling continued, they realized something was terribly wrong. Within hours, Ryan's neck had swollen so much that it pushed his head over against his left shoulder. What's more, his temperature shot up to 105 degrees. Rushed by ambulance to Riley Hospital for Children in Indianapolis, Ryan's condition only worsened.

The infection was being caused by streptococcus bacteria, which had invaded one of Ryan's chicken pox. At that point, the swelling had so severely twisted Ryan's neck that doctors were afraid it would break and damage his spinal column. Believing the infection had entered Ryan's bones, doctors wanted to operate so they could scrape the infection from Ryan's vertebrae and insert pins to hold everything together. Still, they were certain Ryan would not survive the surgery. They also knew he would not survive without surgery. Concluding there was nothing left to do but wait, they fully expected Ryan to die from a broken neck.

Alone with Ryan in his hospital room, Cheryl wept over the realization that her son was dying. There had been another Ryan, years ago, but he'd died too. Ryan Updyke wasn't actually Cheryl's brother, but he might as well have been. The little boy had been just three years old—and Cheryl seven—when he became part of her family. The son of Cheryl's mother's best friend, a single mom who worked evenings, Ryan spent most afternoons and evenings at Cheryl's home. When he was sixteen, Ryan was diagnosed with bone cancer. He died eighteen months later.

When Cheryl and Jeff married and had their first baby, they named him after the "little brother" Cheryl had loved and lost. Cheryl's son didn't know about the young man whose name he shared. She had been looking forward to telling him about the older Ryan one day. Now it seemed that day would never come. And yet it felt like hope was draining away with every passing hour.

Cheryl saw Jeff's Bible lying open on a nearby table. Picking it up, she read Psalm 91:11: "For he will command his angels concerning you to guard you in all your ways." Sobbing, she began to pray. Through her tears, she prayed, "Lord, send four of Your angels to guard the four corners of this room. Watch over my son, protect him, comfort him if he's in any pain, and guide him home to You if he's not going to stay here with us."

The following night, it was Cheryl's turn to stay home with Jordan while Jeff spent the night by Ryan's side. The next morning, Cheryl phoned Jeff. She could hardly utter the words "Good morning" before her husband said, "You need to get down here right away."

When Cheryl walked into Ryan's hospital room, he opened his eyes—mere slits in his still-swollen face—and called out, "Hi, Mommy!" Ryan's doctor turned to Jeff and Cheryl and said, "Well, things are turning around. Thank God we didn't take him into surgery! Let's just see how he does." Ryan's swelling continued to subside by the hour. He was still weak, but recovering quickly.

One day when he'd been home about a week, Cheryl said, "Ryan, you were so, so sick!" They talked about his stay in the hospital. She was thankful he remembered nothing from the first ten days when he was either in excruciating pain or unconscious.

"I prayed for you, Ryan," his mother said. "I prayed for angels to watch over you and help you not feel bad."

"Yeah, I know," he answered.

She looked at him quizzically. "What do you mean, you know?"

"I know," he said. "I saw the angels."

Cheryl glanced at her son. "Really? Where were the angels, Ryan? What did they look like?"

Ryan said matter-of-factly, "They were standing in the corners of the room. And flying around too. There were mommy and daddy ones, and baby ones and grandma and grandpa ones. They were yellow and white and really pretty."

Cheryl didn't know what to think. She half-believed him. Then again, maybe through his coma, he'd heard her praying. "I had a dream too," Ryan said as he hopped around the table. "About Jesus. We were planting stuff in a garden. He said I was a good boy and that He loved me." She looked at her son in wonder. "That's interesting. Anything else?" Ryan was getting fidgety now. He'd sat for too long and was ready to play.

He started skipping toward the door. Cheryl turned back to her mirror. But he stopped and said over his shoulder, "Oh yeah. Ryan says 'Hi.'"

The Tall Visitor

Ingrid Shelton

IT WAS CHRISTMAS EVE, BUT I was not aware of that special day. Lying in a hospital bed in Germany, I'd hovered between life and death for two days.

As refugees after World War II fleeing the Communist regime, my mother, sister, and I had tried to get across the border from East to West Germany. After two nights, we were successful and, on the West German side, we met with Red Cross workers. They placed us with a farm family in a north German village.

Sick from malnutrition and from walking across the border that cold fall night, I developed pleurisy and pneumonia shortly after arriving at our destination. So I was rushed to a city hospital in Oldenburg some miles away.

Now I lay unconscious in bed, my body wracked with fever. The doctor held out no hope of my recovery. Somehow the doctor had connected with neighbors of the farm family by phone, asking them to let my mother know I would not survive the night.

I did not realize how severe my illness was. Earlier that day, I had awakened briefly when I had heard a Christmas carol sung somewhere down the hall. But then I had lapsed again into unconsciousness.

During the night I woke suddenly. A tall, gangly man stood by my bed extending his hand toward me. Even though I did not know him, without question I immediately jumped up and stood next to him. Somehow I knew he had something to do with death.

Up to that time I had been terrified of death. I'd heard of dead people appearing to taunt the living, and I didn't know what would happen to me if I died. I was only ten years old and did not want to think about death.

But as I went to the man, I did not experience any type of emotion. I was neither afraid nor sad.

That tall man took me by the hand, and we moved toward the wall. Yet there didn't seem to be a wall. We floated through at least two more rooms and hallways as if the thick walls did not exist until we arrived at a courtyard outside. That courtyard was surrounded by three hospital wings four stories high. Still clad in my hospital gown and barefoot, I did not feel the cold even though snow and frost blanketed the ground.

Suddenly, we heard an authoritative voice coming from somewhere above. The man and I stopped instantly.

"Don't take her. Take him!" The voice commanded. My eyes focused on the second floor window of one of the wings. I knew that's where the farm family's neighbor boy was hospitalized with diphtheria.

Immediately, the man let go of my hand, grasped my shoulder, and bent my upper body for just a moment. As I bounced back upright, the man disappeared, and I found myself back in my hospital bed.

The next morning, my fever was gone. I was still weak, but I started to recover quickly. My mother rode to the hospital with the neighbor whose son had diphtheria; she was overjoyed to find me alive and almost well.

"Our neighbor's son died suddenly on Christmas Eve night," she told me.

"I know," I said. I was sure the tall man had gone to get the neighbor's son after he let go of me, so the boy's death was not a surprise for me. Yet, somehow I could not tell my mother about my Christmas Eve just then. Would she think I had dreamed or hallucinated?

"The neighbors are devastated. They were told the day before that he was recovering," my mother continued. "And you were so sick. I tried to get to the hospital, but no buses or trains were running. And no taxis were available. I stayed up all night worrying about you. I asked our landlord to hitch up the horse to take me to the hospital, but he said the roads were too icy. I am so glad that you have recovered so quickly. It really is a miracle."

"Yes," I nodded, thinking about the Christmas Eve night in the courtyard. Who was the man who came to get me that night? And whose was the authoritative voice we had heard in the courtyard?

I had never heard of God or of the Bible.

Just before I was discharged, I took a walk through the hospital and came to a courtyard. I was astonished to recognize it as the one the man had taken me to. Suddenly I knew beyond a shadow of a doubt that my experience on Christmas Eve had been real not a hallucination.

Years went by. Later on in life I finally learned that God was real. Through that hospital experience God had taught me not only that there is life after death, but also that He is in control of the universe. His plan for me was to stay on earth at that time. I realized it was God's voice the angel and I had heard in the hospital courtyard on that Christmas Eve night.

Just like God had sent Jesus to die in my place so that I might have eternal life, I feel the young neighbor's son was taken into eternity in my place for reasons I cannot know now. It is a lesson I will always remember. I am grateful that I had another chance at life that Christmas Eve, grateful that God gave me opportunities to share the story of His grace in my life with those around me.

A Glimpse of Heaven's Glory

Janet Franck

I DON'T KNOW WHY TRAGEDY struck our family that bright October morning. Nor why I, of all people, should have been allowed that glimpse of glory. I only know that a presence greater than human was part of the experience from the beginning.

The strangeness started the evening before, when I allowed six-year-old Travis to play outside past his bedtime. I'd never done this before. Travis's two younger brothers were already asleep in bed, and he should have been too; he had to go to school in the morning, after all. But Tara, the little girl who lived across the street, was playing outdoors late too. Though Tara was a year older, there seemed to be a special bond between her and Travis. I heard their happy shouts as they played hide-and-seek under the enormous stars—just as I used to here in our little mountain town of Challis, Idaho.

And then, later, when I'd called him in at last and he was in his pajamas, he'd suddenly grown so serious...

"Mommy?" Travis had finished his prayers as I sat on the edge of his bed. He took his hands and placed them tenderly on my cheeks. Such a solemn little face beneath the freckles!

"What, Babe?" I smiled.

"I...just love you, Mommy," he said, searching my eyes. "I just want you to know that I love you."

The words remained with me as I got ready for bed. Not that it was unusual for Travis to show affection. His outgoing nature had become even more so after he accepted Jesus as his Savior, at age five. Little children who know Jesus seem to bubble over with love for the whole world. It was the intensity—almost the urgency—with which he'd said the words that was unlike him.

As I lay in bed that night, the sense that something out of the ordinary was about to happen stayed with me. Our house is small, and since my mother came to stay with us I've shared a bedroom with the children. I could hear their soft, restful breaths as they slept. That wasn't what kept me awake. Nor was it the empty space beside me—my husband was now married to another. Yes, our family had certainly had its moments of pain, but our faith had brought us this far.

I thought back to that time, four years before, when I'd realized my need for the Savior and invited Him to take over my struggle. How magnificently He had! So much help had been lavished upon us going through the divorce, the changed lifestyle, and the financial difficulties. From our pastor and church friends I'd gained strength and hope. But it was the conversion of little freckle-faced Travis that brought me the day-by-day lessons.

"Why are you worried, Mommy?" Travis had said so many times, a hint of impatience in his wide brown eyes. "You have Jesus. We'll get the money for that bill." And we always did.

Two AM. "I love you, Mommy" still pealed in my ears like some distant, gentle bell. I remembered that as my closeness to Jesus increased, my spirit would sometimes hear messages from Him.

I am preparing Travis for something, I'd heard this silent voice tell me, many times. And this did seem to be the case. Hadn't there been that night a couple of months ago...? I'd awaked before daylight and noticed Travis sitting on his bed...just sitting, in the purple predawn.

"What's the matter, Babe?" I had asked him.

"Don't you see them?" He sounded disappointed.

"See what?"

"These two angels."

I breathed in sharply; I saw only the familiar room. The boy was wide-awake, perfectly calm. I asked him if he was afraid.

"No, Mommy," he'd said. I waited by his bed a little while. Then he said, "Okay, they're gone, you can go to bed now." That was all. But thinking back on that experience, I felt again that sense of the extraordinary pressing close upon us.

The morning of October 28 dawned bright and still. There was the usual bustle of getting breakfast, finding socks that matched, pencils with erasers and so on. Ten minutes before the time he usually left to walk to school Travis became suddenly agitated:

"Mommy, I've got to go now."

"Babe, it's early. You've got lots of time. Sit down."

"I've got to go now! I've just got to!" Travis cried.

"Why?" I asked in bewilderment. He mumbled something about his teacher, about not being late. It didn't make sense: He was never late. "Wait a few minutes," I insisted. "Finish your cocoa."

"Mommy, please!" To my amazement big tears were rolling down his cheeks.

"All right, all right, go ahead," I told him, shaking my head at the commotion. He dashed out the door, a hurrying little figure pulling on a tan jacket. Across the street, little Tara was coming down her walk. I saw the two children meet and set off toward Main Street together.

Five minutes later I was clearing away the breakfast dishes when it happened. A shudder of the floor beneath me, then a hideous screech of writhing wood. There had never been an earthquake in Challis, but I knew we were having an earthquake now. I ran from the house calling over my shoulder, "I've got to get to Travis!"

I was at the driveway when another tremor flung me against the car. I waited till the earth stopped heaving, then climbed into the driver's seat.

I'd gone two blocks when I saw a woman standing beside a pile of rubble on the sidewalk, the debris of a collapsed storefront. The look on her face was one of nightmare horror. Unrolling the window, I was surprised at the calmness of my voice as I asked, "Was someone...caught?"

"Two children," the white face said thinly. "One in a tan jacket..."

I drove swiftly on. Past people running toward the damaged building. Around the corner. To the school. Oh, I knew. I knew already. But maybe (please God!), maybe farther down the street there'd be two children standing bewildered at a curbside. There were not, of course. I drove back to the rubble heap.

Then a numb blur of events: police, firemen, people struggling with the debris. Identification. Arms around me. I was at the clinic. I was being driven home. I was in my living room again. My mother was there, and I was telling her and my two little boys what had happened. Mother was praying.

Suddenly, as I sat there in the living room, perhaps even in mid-sentence—I don't know how long it took—I was being lifted right out of the room, lifted above it all, high into the sky, and placed by a beautiful gate. A cluster of happy people stood within the gate. In utter amazement I began recognizing the youthful, robust faces: Dad, my favorite aunt, Grandpa...and in the center of them all, the radiant form of Jesus! As I watched, He stretched out His hands to welcome a child who was approaching, a smiling boy dressed in what seemed to be an unbleached muslin tunic over long trousers of the same homespun-looking fabric. Travis ran forward and grasped the hand of Jesus, looking up at Him with eager brown eyes. The cluster of people welcomed my son, and he seemed to recognize them, although some he had never met. As the joyful group turned to leave, Travis suddenly turned his shining face toward me.

"It's really neat here, Mommy."

"I know, Babe." My throat felt choked, and I don't know whether I spoke out loud or not.

"I really like it here."

"I know."

"Mommy...I don't want to go back."

"It's okay, Babe." And it was okay, in that transcendent moment. Nothing I could ever do, nothing that could ever happen here on earth, could make Travis as happy as I saw him right then. When I looked around me, I was back in my home.

That's where the long battle of grief was fought, of course: in the kitchen with its empty chair, in the bedroom where he'd said his goodnight prayers, and the yard where he'd played hide-and-seek. Transcendent moments do not last—not for us on earth. Three years have passed since the day of the earthquake, passed among the daily routines of cleaning, cooking, chauffeuring, praying.

But neither do such moments fade. That scene at heaven's threshold is as vivid in each detail today as in the measureless instant when I was allowed to see. I have been granted another glimpse since then, this time of Tara among a group of joyfully playing children, all dressed in those tunic-like garments. (I did not see Travis this time, nor anyone else I recognized.)

Tara's mother understands no better than I the why of a child's death, the why of heaven's glory. I know only that both are real, and that—when we hear the answer at last—it will start with the words, "I love you."

Bagpipes in Heaven

James L. Garlow & Keith Wall

RALPH WAS LUCKY TO BE alive. An aneurism that had formed in the wall of his left ventricle could have ruptured at any moment and killed him. Surgery was imperative—and soon. He was referred to a specialist, Dr. David Heimansohn, who was using a unique revascularization technique that showed good results in cases featuring severe damage. This seemingly routine connection would turn out to be anything *but.*

Ralph was admitted to St. Vincent's Hospital and spent a quiet night awaiting surgery. His thoughts predictably were filled with uncertainty, but the outlook was good.

The Saturday procedure was a success. Dr. Heimansohn left with his family immediately afterward for a much-deserved break at his vacation home in Michigan. Though Ralph remained in the ICU, all signs pointed to an uneventful recovery.

Then came the evening crash. Ralph's blood pressure bottomed out, and he hovered perilously close to cardiac arrest—another way of saying "near death," defined as a heart's complete shutdown. His grip on life was slipping, and there was little the staff could do to strengthen it. Now the prognosis was so grim, Ralph's wife, Sue, decided to call extended family members, who made plans to travel through the night to be present in the increasingly likely event of Ralph's death.

"I was in and out of consciousness," he said. "I only remember bits and pieces, but I do recall the pain—and the thirst. I was purposely dehydrated to lower the volume of blood in my body and take the load off my heart. Every time I woke, the sensation of thirst was horrible, very intense."

Sunday morning, Ralph heard distant music. He wondered who was playing music in the ICU of all places. As it grew louder, he recognized the sound of bagpipes, playing a tune strangely familiar, like something he'd heard in a forgotten dream or encountered so long ago that it was more an impression than a memory.

He was about to ask a nurse about this when the worst happened: His heart stopped beating. Cardiac arrest. Technically, Ralph died.

The staff launched into hyperactivity to mount resuscitation, knowing they had only minutes to succeed. The object of their frantic attention was entirely unaware of it.

"Suddenly, I'm standing on a grassy hilltop," Ralph recalled. "I feel fit and strong and wide awake. A lush green meadow rolls downward and away in front of me. To my left stands an old stone wall that follows the contour of the meadow into the valley below. On the right I see a rocky ocean shoreline, with waves breaking gently on gray boulders. The sky is a vibrant, vivid blue, and a refreshing breeze carries the scent of grass and rich earth."

At that moment, Ralph felt as lucid as he'd ever been. The images around him didn't seem surreal, as they often do in a typical dream state. He had no doubt he was truly there, wherever that might be. The music was powerful and loud now, and Ralph saw "a man of small stature" strolling away from him down the hill, dressed in a kilt and playing the bagpipes. The song was a pleasant "Irish-sounding" ballad he was certain he'd heard before. Voices sang the melody as the man walked and played.

The scene before him—coupled with his new sensation of vital well-being—filled Ralph with overwhelming peace and joy, like nothing he'd experienced on earth. In an instant he grasped beyond doubt the overwhelming intensity of God's love for him and for the world.

"It's impossible to describe with words what I felt," he said. "Happiness and contentment times thousands and thousands. I remember thinking, *This is what I've been looking for all my life. Everything I've ever done, good or bad, was a step on my journey to this place. All that came before was my attempt to find my way here.*"

Over the next several hours, Ralph "died" and was revived (shocked back) ten times. Each time his heart stopped, he found himself on the same hillside, watching the man walk away from him as he played the wonderful music. Ralph had a burning desire to follow but instinctively knew that if he did he'd be unable to return to life as he'd known it. He was torn between wanting to stay and feelings of responsibility for his wife and children.

"I can't come now," he said out loud to the man. "I'll come with you later."

The following day, Ralph was awake, with both his blood pressure and heart rate stabilized. Seven months later he received a heart transplant.

What to make of the fellow he met in heaven?

"When my mother heard what had happened, she swore the man with the bagpipes was my grandfather come to lead me to heaven," he recalled. "I don't know what any of the images I saw really mean: the man, the hillside, the ocean. The truth is I don't care. What matters to me is that intense feeling of love, peace, and happiness. I really believe what I experienced was just a tiny bit of God's love."

Twin Angels

Bruce Van Natta

IT WAS A BIG JOB, the kind I loved. There aren't many people who know how to tear down and rebuild the engine on a Peterbilt logging truck. I'd built my mechanic business from scratch and was proud of what I'd accomplished. Across central Wisconsin I was the guy to call for heavy machinery repairs.

On this particular November day I was finishing up work on an engine at the truck owner's garage. I'd spent most of the last three days removing the head gasket and cylinder head, carefully disassembling clamps, cables and other engine parts. It took a lot of horses to power this big boy. The front wheels and axle alone carried over eleven thousand pounds. Now, in the home stretch of a twelve-hour day, my mind kept returning to a discussion my wife, Lori, and I had two nights ago about our faith. I wasn't sure where she was coming from. God had already changed me so much, helped me overcome problems with drugs and alcohol. And He had given me this talent to fix engines and a successful business. Yet Lori believed I could deepen my faith still more, meeting God in my life in ways I had yet to understand.

I filled the engine with oil and coolant then started it to make sure everything was in running order. Almost done. I was putting away my tools when the truck driver and part-time mechanic asked if I'd look at an oil leak unrelated to my work. "Sure," I said.

The passenger-side wheel was removed and the jack was still in place. I slid under the truck feet first on a creeper. Peering into the underside of the rumbling engine, I wiped away oil with a rag, trying to find the leak. As I looked up, I saw some movement in my peripheral vision, turning my head just in time to see the jack shoot out from under the front axle like a rocket. Before I could react, the axle slammed across my midsection, crushing me to the floor. I screamed in agony till I was gasping for air, my lungs burning. Then a final involuntary cry from deep inside me: "God, help me!" My arms strained against the axle. It didn't budge. My arms collapsed, the pain too intense. Sweat soaked my face and hair. The engine rumbled, each vibration grinding the axle down on me. I heard the other mechanic calling 911. "Hurry! He's smashed under the truck."

It's too late. I'm going to die. I tasted blood, felt it running down my chin. The mechanic turned off the engine. Then he began jacking up the truck again. The axle slowly rose off me, but the pain didn't let up. I reached back and grabbed the bottom of the front bumper with my hands to pull myself out. But I moved less than a foot before my muscles collapsed, only enough for my head to stick out from the bottom of the truck.

I thought about Lori and the kids. I loved them so much. I wished I could see them to tell them good-bye. But everything was fading. Turning black.

The next thing I knew it was as if I were watching a movie from fifteen feet in the air, a scene unfolding below me, the logging truck in the foreground. A man's head stuck out from beneath the front of the truck, another man on his knees by him, stroking his hair.

"Hang on," said the kneeling man. "I don't want to move you. The paramedics are coming. Please don't die." The man under the truck was me…I was watching myself.

Intrigued, I looked closer. Was I alive? There was no sign of movement. I realized the pain was gone. Now I felt nothing. No, this can't be the end. I shut my eyes tight, trying to will myself back into my body. I opened my eyes again. No. I was still watching myself from above. But wait…there below me were two incredible figures kneeling on either side of the other mechanic. I knew what they were—angels. They were like no angels I'd ever imagined—massive, powerful men, bigger than any NFL linebacker. I could see only their backs. They wore radiant, white robes made from some type of heavy material, almost as if it were woven from ropes. Curly blond hair fell halfway down their backs. Their arms reached under the truck toward my crushed midsection.

God had sent angels! Their presence filled the garage in a supernatural way. But watching from above it seemed natural, inviting. I wanted to feel their touch, to see their faces. Is this what happens when you die?

I saw a paramedic rush into the garage, seemingly oblivious to the angels. She knelt on the floor next to my head, the angels not moving. She was talking to me as I watched from above. Then she tapped me on the cheek—hard. My face! I could feel again! In the distance I heard a voice getting louder. "Open your eyes!" When I did, I was looking up—into the eyes of the paramedic. "Hello, Bruce," she said. "Keep those eyes open for me. It's very important."

I was alive! I looked to my right and left. The angels were gone. Excruciating pain ripped through my body. Where were the angels? Why had they left? I felt myself fading again, something telling me to let go. I didn't have the strength to push back. Then a clear, powerful voice: "If you want to live, I'm here," it said. "But it won't be easy. You're going to have to fight, harder than you've ever fought for anything. Are you willing?" It wasn't an angel speaking, or the paramedic. It was God's voice speaking deep inside me, deeper than the pain. I'd have to fight. But not alone.

My mind flashed on an image of Lori and the kids. I thought of how much they needed me. No, that wasn't right. I needed them, especially now. *God*, I prayed, *I want to live. I want to fight for them and for You. I'll do whatever it takes.*

More paramedics, urgently discussing how they'd move me. Slowly they pulled the creeper out from under the truck. "We're going to take you to the hospital now," the first paramedic said. "From there you'll be airlifted to the trauma center in Madison. We've contacted your wife. She'll meet you there. I know you're hurting, but stay with me. You're doing great." For the next hour—till we reached the trauma center—I focused with all my strength on keeping my eyes open. Keep looking around. As long as you can see, you're alive.

The doctors at the trauma center rushed me to the operating room. I have a vague memory of the anesthesia mask covering my nose and mouth. Then all went dark, as dark as death.

The next thing I remember is looking through a kind of haze. Lori was sitting beside me. Even in my stupor I could see the huge smile on her face. "Bruce! You're awake! The doctors have had you in a coma for two weeks. They said to cross my fingers. I told them I was going to pray. I've never said so many prayers!" I wanted to talk, but a breathing tube filled my mouth. I wanted to write, but my arms were too weak to move. It was another week, the second week of December, before the doctor removed the tube and I could tell Lori everything. "Something happened to me," I said.

"It's okay," she said. "The accident. You've had three surgeries. Don't push yourself. You don't need to talk."

"No," I said. "I need to tell you. It's about our discussion. You were right. God has something He needs me to do. I know He'll help me figure it out. Lori, I saw angels after the truck fell on me. He sent angels to save me!"

"Even the doctors said it was a miracle you survived," she said. "Rest now." I nodded weakly. There'd be plenty of time. The future stretched before me like a blank page, inviting me to write a new chapter. God had sent angels to let me know He'd be there with me through the challenges ahead, that my relationship with Him would deepen. That was the promise of the angels.

Doctors operated on me twice more—literally putting my insides back together. It was months more before the pain subsided enough for me to function. Today, I travel around the world, sharing my story in churches, jails, schools, and on the Internet. I've even written a book. The accident has changed my life forever. I've learned how frail the human body is. Yet I've discovered the strength the Lord offers us to draw from, present in ways I could never have believed.

August Awakening

Marie Cleary

I COULDN'T WAIT TO GET into the ocean. My sister, Peggy, and I ran ahead of our parents, dashing up the Clark Street ramp to the boardwalk. We threaded through the crowd, bumping into the adults, craning our necks to see the beach through their legs and knees.

"Slow down, Marie," Daddy shouted. He set up the big beach umbrella while my mother, aunt, and grandmother spread out on the baking sand. I stripped off my shorts and sandals and followed Peggy into the water. It rushed up over my bare feet. "Catch me!" Peggy shouted, splashing me. I ran after her, giggling, until a big wave picked us both off our feet and sent us tumbling—soaked—back to shore. "Be careful!" my father shouted from his blanket. "Those waves are mighty big today." Daddy was the disciplinarian of the family, but even he couldn't slow us down. Peggy and I were having much too much fun to listen.

My family always spent August at the beach in Wildwood, New Jersey, where my Aunt Ethel owned a boarding house. After dinner, we'd go for a walk on the boardwalk. I'd hold my mother's hand, staring up at the bright neon lights over the movie theaters and the arcades. It was like peeking into a different world. Then there was the ocean. I could smell the saltwater everywhere I went and hear the faint pounding of the surf, almost drowned out by the music from the merry-go-round and the roar of the wooden roller coaster. All year long I looked forward to August. The beach was my favorite place on earth.

Peggy and I played in the waves until our fingers were wrinkled from the saltwater. "I'm getting out," Peggy declared. "I'm hungry."

"Five more minutes," I begged her. I knew Daddy wouldn't let me stay in the water alone. But Peggy was already running up the beach. I hesitated, wondering whether I should follow her. I don't know what happened next. I never saw the wave that hit me—never even heard it. One moment I was standing in water up to my waist, the next I was under the water. My feet couldn't find the ground. I opened my mouth to scream and choked instead. The current pulled me and spun me through darkness. I squeezed my eyes shut, certain that I was going to die. Daddy always said that was it, when you die, you die. Death was the end.

I couldn't breathe. My lungs burned. Everything went still. I was sitting cross-legged on the cold, hard sand of the ocean floor, breathing in and out. I wasn't afraid. I felt good. I touched my bathing suit. It was dry. How could that be? I looked around. The water was murky and dark, but I could see flat stones, tangled seaweed, stiff ridges in the sand. In the distance was a pinpoint of white light as bright as a star. That must be the way out, I thought.

I crawled toward the light on my hands and knees. As I got closer, I saw a ladder in the sand—an old-fashioned wooden ladder painted shiny white. It stretched up for a long way, disappearing into the light. I put my foot on the bottom rung. It seemed solid. Hand over hand, I climbed. The farther I climbed, the greater the space between the rungs. I had to stretch my whole body to reach the next one, pulling myself up with all my strength. I was panting by the time I reached the top. But what was this? I'd come to a small room, like a waiting room, with benches on either side. Empty benches. If only someone would tell me where to go. A door stood open at the far end of the room. That's where the light was coming from. Shielding my eyes, I stumbled toward it and collapsed at the entrance. I lay on my stomach, halfway across the threshold. The light was so brilliant, I couldn't lift my eyes. I stared at the ground in front of me.

What I saw surprised me. Feet. Lots and lots of bare feet. Hundreds of people walking back and forth. I could make out the hems of their white robes. It was like peering through the crowd at the boardwalk. I knew there was something exciting on the other side, something I wanted to see. Something just beyond my reach. Like what Grandma said about heaven. When Dad wasn't around, Grandma told me a different story about death. She said it was a beginning. Of a new life where we'd live with God in heaven. The way Grandma talked about heaven made me think that one day I'd like it even more than the beach in August. *God, is this the heaven Grandma tried to tell me about?* I began to push myself into the room, but a voice called out, "You can't come in." Gripping the door frame, I raised myself up on my knees. I squeezed my eyes shut and felt a warm shiver rush through my whole body. Then a hand grabbed mine. I plunged forward. Searing pain gripped my lungs. I gagged.

"Take it easy." *Daddy!* I felt his strong arms cradling me before I opened my eyes. I was back on the beach. Mom, Peggy, Grandma, Aunt Ethel—they all crowded around as Dad laid me out on a towel. He slapped my back, and I went into a fit of coughing.

"We looked everywhere," Mom was saying. "Thank goodness Daddy saw your hand reaching out of the surf. What were you doing?"

It all came back: the bright light, the ladder, the doorway, all those people on the other side.

"I…I don't know," I managed to say. How would they believe me if I didn't know what to believe myself?

For the rest of the afternoon, I drank cold spring water and dozed under the shade of the umbrella. After the scare, my family relaxed. Peggy was even swimming again. No one knew how close I had come to dying. No one but me. Those vivid images circled in my mind: the light, the ladder, the beckoning door. Had I seen Grandma's heaven?

The sun began to set, and my mother rolled up the blankets. It was time to go home. Before we left, Daddy took my hand and led me down to the water. A shiver ran through me as I looked at the breaking waves. "I want you to go in," he said. I stared at my feet, not budging an inch. "What are you afraid of?"

I hesitated, then blurted out the whole story, tears streaming down my cheeks. "I was in heaven, Daddy," I told him. "I really was!"

"Heaven isn't real," he said. "Only this is real. This beach, this earth, this life. Promise me that you will never ever tell anyone that silly story again."

As the sun sank below the horizon, I stepped into the waves. And for so long, I kept my promise to Daddy. I never told a soul about my vision. Not my mother or grandmother, not my husband, not my closest friend. Still, hardly a day went by that I didn't think of it. God had planted a seed in my heart that day at the beach, a seed of faith. And it grew until I could no longer deny the truth. There is a heaven waiting for us beyond the sun setting over the ocean. A heaven more beautiful than the beach in August.

CHAPTER 4

Mysterious Knowings

Kitchen Angel

Susan Karas

BRUCE HAD MADE BIG SACRIFICES to buy me a diamond engagement ring, and what had I done? Lost it. I stood in our kitchen staring at the now empty prongs. Where could that diamond have fallen out? My mind raced with possibilities. Being a newlywed was hard enough—maintaining the house, learning to live together, making compromises. I couldn't face telling Bruce I'd lost the most expensive thing he'd ever gotten me. I looked out the kitchen window. *I need help, Lord. I've got to find that diamond.*

I searched the yard. I retraced my steps around the kitchen and walked through the living room. Nothing. I came back to the kitchen empty-handed. What could I do but tell Bruce. I flicked some breadcrumbs off the counter. Some newlywed I was.

"Wipe them up!"

I reeled around. *Who said that?* I was alone in the house. And so upset it seemed my mind was playing tricks on me. But it was true: I shouldn't have just flicked those crumbs. The least I could do was to keep a clean house—especially after losing my diamond.

~ *131* ~

I swept the dish sponge across the counter and wiped up the crumbs. I turned on the faucet to rinse the sponge off in the sink. But something glinted on the sponge. A glittery crumb? Peering closer, my jaw dropped. There, caught in the groove on the sponge was my precious diamond.

I danced around the kitchen, the happiest newlywed on earth. This bride had a kitchen angel, always at her side.

"Pull In"

Jackie Osinski

WE LIVE ON A SMALL farm in Indiana with a few horses, cats, and chickens. My daughters each have their own horse and often enter horse shows or just spend the day with their dad riding out in the forest. One particular day my oldest daughter decided to go trail-riding with her dad out in Pekin, a small rural town that is surrounded by hundreds of acres of forestry and riding trails. They spent the day running the horses with friends, exploring new trails, and just enjoying the cool September weather. I hadn't heard from them all day as was normal when they were out having a good time. At about 5:00 PM my cell phone rang. It was Michael.

"Jackie, Cowboy is severely injured, and I can't load him into the trailer. The only way for me to get him home is to walk him."

I gripped the receiver tightly. "What? What happened? Are you and Nicky okay?"

"We were done riding for the day when we decided to load the horses up and head home. We loaded the palomino up with no problem. When it came time to load Cowboy he was skittish as usual. Just when I was about to get him into the trailer a person walked behind him, and he reared up. His head hit the top of the trailer and as he came down he tore off the skin from his ears down to his nose. It was just a flap hanging off his nose."

Cowboy was an appendix; half quarter horse, half thoroughbred, making him very skittish and nervous about doing anything new. Being loaded into a trailer was one of the most difficult things to get Cowboy to do.

"How did you fix the injuries?" I asked nervously.

"I had some paper towels and duct tape. I held up the flap of skin and taped up his forehead. It's bleeding pretty badly. Everyone has left the riding area. I can't take a chance of trying to load him up. I need you to pick up Nicky and the palomino. I am going to walk Cowboy back home."

I shook my head. "Michael, there's a huge storm coming. It's already starting to get dark. That's a fourteen-mile walk home. How are you going to make it with a severely injured horse?"

"Listen to me, Jackie," Michael said quickly. "Come get the horse trailer. I will do the best I can to make it home before it gets dark."

I started shaking. The only way to Pekin was through a very high, winding, and hilly country road. It is very difficult to maneuver in a car, not to mention during a storm walking an injured horse. I grabbed the car keys and drove the thirty minutes it took to get to the riding trails. When I finally pulled up, the sky was already turning a dark, muddy gray. Michael had already started walking through the woods to save time on the road. Nicky was standing beside the trailer with her horse already loaded. We jumped in the truck and slowly began to make our way down the long, winding incline.

As I drove, I noticed the dark blood blotches on Nicky's jeans and sleeves. She looked out the truck window, exhausted. We both knew it would be hours before Michael would make it back to the farm. Coming upon a turn in the road I saw them. Michael was walking on the side of the road holding Cowboy with a lead line. I pulled over. Cowboy's head was soaked with blood. The duct tape was matted with hair and dried blood.

I pleaded with Michael, "Please stop. You'll never make it. The storm is going to hit us any minute now." Just then I saw a flash of lighting out of the corner of my eye.

"Listen to me, Jackie. This is the only way I can get Cowboy home safely. Just take care of yourselves and pray the weather holds up."

I was a complete mess. There was nothing I could do but pray. The first words that came out of my mouth were, "Lord, send me an angel."

I repeated those words over and over. Each time I took another hairpin turn with the horse trailer, I prayed, "Lord, send me an angel."

One mile passed, then two. Drops of rain began to fall and the winds started blowing. "Lord, send me an angel."

I had just spoken those words again when I came upon a small, white farmhouse. "*Pull in.*" The words came clear as a bell.

Pulling into the driveway I noticed a man sitting in the backyard with his dog on his lap. Slowly, peacefully, they rocked back and forth. Running to him, I poured out our plight. Finally, I said, "Sir, I don't know if you can help but we are in a desperate situation."

With a long drawl he said, "Well, I just happen to break and train horses. Soon as your husband comes down this corner, we'll see what we can do."

Suddenly a gentle breeze of peace overtook me. His tranquil, assuring manner made me relax instantly. I took a deep breath. Twenty minutes passed before Michael came down off the hilly pass. Looking at Cowboy and Michael, I could see that they were both exhausted. The blood was continuing to run down Cowboy's forehead. Running to Michael, I quickly explained what had just happened. I told him that my only prayer was "Lord, please send an angel."

"Michael, I believe that this man is our answer to prayer."

Large drops of rain were now falling. Thunder was rolling over our heads. As Michael walked Cowboy onto the driveway, our new friend said, "Mind if I hold him a minute?"

Cowboy seemed to relax in this man's presence. He spoke softly to the horse as he walked him around in circles a few times. After about five minutes of this, he opened the trailer door, pulled the lead line up around the horse's rump and gently pulled Cowboy inside. Smiling, the gentleman locked the gate and said, "There, your horse will be fine now. You all better head home before the storm hits."

With many words of thanks, we all jumped into the truck and headed home. No, our angel didn't come with wings or a halo, but he provided the supernatural help an injured horse needed on a stormy night.

It was exactly what I had been praying for.

What Billy Knew

Etril Leinbach

PASTORING A RURAL CHURCH IN the 1950s and '60s meant earning most of your living doing something else. For fifteen years, I drove a school bus, and so did my wife, Wilma. We lived near Three Rivers in southwestern Michigan, named for the rivers that meet in the center of town—the Rocky, the Portage and the St. Joseph.

My church for twenty years was the Moore Park Mennonite Church, about five miles from Three Rivers. Looking back at those years, I see that our life was filled with children—our own three boys and the children of Moore Park and Three Rivers.

Early every weekday morning we picked them up and drove them to the community school, and in the afternoon we loaded them up again and took them home. We knew everyone. If teachers wondered where a child lived, they asked Wilma and me.

I have so many memories of those kids, but there's one I remember especially. His name was Billy Misel. I first saw him in 1962, when he boarded my bus on the day he started kindergarten. He was a quiet child, and tall for his age even then. I saw him most school days into sixth grade, and each summer when he enrolled in the Bible school at my church.

One day in 1968, Billy's sixth-grade teacher gave the class a writing assignment. Billy decided to write about his dream from the night before: An angel had come to him and had taken him to heaven. Billy saw mansions and streets of gold, angels and the throne of God. Heaven seemed to be a wonderful place. The angel told Billy he could live there, but he would have to go back to earth for seven days. After that time, the angel would come for him, and he could live in heaven with God and His angels forever.

Billy had always been a serious boy, and the dream affected him deeply. The image of heaven was beautiful, and he liked thinking about it. He described his dream on paper and then read the story to his classmates. Seven days later he was riding with his brother in a pickup truck. There was an accident, and Billy was killed.

A call came from the Misel family after Billy's death, and I went to their home to make preparations for the funeral. I expected to pray with them and to express my own grief. How can anyone be prepared when the life of someone so young is ended so abruptly? But I did not yet know of Billy's school assignment. His mother asked me to sit down, and she gave me the paper to read—Billy's story of his dream, the story of his angel, written in his own hand.

At Billy's funeral, I read his story out loud to a large assemblage of friends, who were profoundly moved by his words. I have described the experience countless times in the years since. It is possible, of course, that the magnificent place he saw was the product of a young boy's imagination, enriched by the Bible stories he heard every summer at my church. It is possible that the angel was just a dream. But I believe Billy was visited by a messenger from heaven so he would not be afraid of what lay ahead, and he shared his vision with us here on earth.

Seven days tell me so.

Four Mysterious Visitors

David Waite

LAST CHRISTMAS GOT OFF TO a promising start. Alison and I and the children—two of our four were still at home—had picked out a tree and its lights were twinkling merrily in the living room. I had lit a fire to take the edge off our raw English air. And then twelve-year-old Matthew hesitantly asked me a question that would have been perfectly natural in any other household: "Dad, would it be all right if I put on some Christmas music?"

"Of course," I said too quickly.

I braced myself. As strains of "Hark! The Herald Angels Sing" began to fill the house, a familiar gnawing sensation grew in the pit of my stomach. *Not again*, I thought. Christmas carols were one of the triggers that could inexplicably bring on a severe anxiety attack. I slipped out of the living room and met Ali in the hallway.

"Are you all right?" she asked. I shrugged. "Do you want to turn off the music?"

"I can't do that," I said. I went upstairs to my office. Work would keep my mind occupied. I tried to focus on a newspaper feature but succeeded only in staring at the impatiently blinking cursor.

I had hoped the old fears would not plague me this Christmas. All my life I had been beset with vague apprehensions and the awful depressions that followed.

The roots weren't hard to find. Born prematurely, forty-nine years ago in the village of Styal near Manchester, I spent the first three months of life fighting to survive. I had been born with a shortened and twisted right leg that, later, made walking difficult. In my first week at school a girl pointed at me. "You're a cripple!" she said. She hobbled off in a perfect imitation of my limp that set the other kids laughing.

Being lame of body was not half as bad, though, as being crippled in spirit. My mental woes may have been inherited. My granddad suffered from free-floating fears and so did my father. Dad was so tense that he and Mum were in constant rows, yelling at each other, slamming doors, hurling crockery, then continuing the battle with silence that could last for weeks.

My first serious depression occurred in my early teens. Dad was the village bobby and on his salary we couldn't afford psychiatric help, even if he had believed in it. Antidepressant drugs were in use by 1960, but I was wary of trying these early experimental medicines.

There were glimmers of hope. I became a Christian at eighteen, and for a while I believed this commitment might help me get better. It didn't—not for more than thirty years. Of course I prayed about my anxieties, always in private because I was far too shy to bring up my need at church.

When I married Alison I hoped I was beginning a new, healthier chapter. But along with the joy of a wife and growing family came responsibilities that made the problem worse. Six weeks was the longest I could go without suffering an acute anxiety attack. Little things set the explosions off. A bill coming due. A Christmas carol. The family was ready to leave for church one summer day when I realized my cuff links were missing. It didn't matter because I was wearing a short-sleeved shirt, but I held us up until the cuff links were found.

I was spoiling things for everyone. The best I could do was keep out of the way while depressed. Soon I was spending days on end in my room, as my family waited for me to come around again.

Then on the fifteenth of December last year, a few days after the renewed battle with Christmas carols, I was putting my good foot, the left one, on a step when I stumbled. Searing pain shot through my leg. Within an hour I could not use the leg at all. It was just the kind of incident that usually sank me into a depressive state. Ali offered to pray not only for the leg pain but also for the funk that would almost certainly follow.

What good would prayer do? We had asked God to help us so often. But this time He was about to answer, and in a fashion I could never have anticipated.

Ali prayed for me and my leg did get better, but not the signs of oncoming depression. That evening, just ten days before Christmas, as we were getting ready for bed, Ali remembered that because of the cold weather she had not opened the windows as she usually did to freshen the room. She picked up what she thought was an air-purifying spray and sent a mist all over the room. But the spray turned out to be a sore-muscle balm with a dreadful menthol smell that I've always hated.

"Whew!" I said. "I'll have to sleep in Daniel's room if I want to get any rest." Our oldest son, Daniel, was in London and his room was empty.

I kissed Ali good night, walked to Daniel's room and turned down the spread on his narrow bed, which was right up against the wall. I climbed in, turned out the light and lay there staring into the darkness. I was unusually warm and comfortable but still fretting about all sorts of things . . . bills, a close friend in hospital, an assignment that was due.

At first, the way you can sometimes sense a person looking at you, it seemed to me someone was in the room, focusing attention on me. I thought Alison had stepped in. "Ali?" I whispered.

There was no answer, not a rustling of clothes, not a stirring of air, and yet I knew beyond doubt I was not alone. A friendly presence was near me, at the head of the bed. Had Daniel come home unexpectedly? I whispered his name. Nothing. Maybe it was one of the younger children. "Matthew? Caroline?" No answer.

Slowly I became aware of a second unseen being in the room, this one at the foot of the bed. It seemed to me the two creatures were facing each other. And then I knew there was a third presence too, and a fourth one, these last two facing each other on the left side of the bed . . . impossible since there was no space between the bed and the wall.

I wanted to call Ali, but there was something so benevolent, so full of promise about the four lively presences that I didn't want to do anything that might risk driving them away. I lay perfectly still, strangely warm and expectant.

And then—how did I know this, since I could not see them?—the four creatures began to move toward one another, two on each side of the bed. Their progress was slow and deliberate. They passed one another, turned and repeated the traverse three, four, maybe five times. Every time their paths crossed I felt as if I would burst with joy.

Then abruptly the room was empty. I knew it as surely as I had known a few minutes earlier that angelic creatures were there. The room was back to normal and I was alone again, yet still filled with ineffable joy. Should I go tell Alison? But tell her what? That I had been visited by four beings I couldn't see? Still debating, I fell into a deep sleep, the best I had had in years.

By the time I surfaced, the children had already left for school. "You'll never believe what happened last night," I said to Ali. I told her as best I could about the mysterious visitors God had sent me. Alison did believe it and was delighted at my newfound joy and peace, though perhaps wondering, as I was, if this calm would last for more than a few days.

Our doubts were misplaced. I enjoyed every minute of the Christmas season. December was followed by a long gray January and February, two months that in the past had been times of distress but were filled with exultation new to me. The joy even survived a devastating bout I had with the flu. Winter gave way to a spring, a summer and then an autumn of freedom.

Though I can't be sure how long this freedom will last, I am beginning to believe the victory is permanent. It's not that I've shed pressures like bills and problems at work. But today I confront these issues with a positive attitude unlike my past fearfulness.

Christmas is once again just around the corner. Thanks to my heavenly visitors, I'm anticipating another joy-filled season and I am going to make a statement to that effect. This year I have bought a present for the entire family, a small but very special gift I hope we will use a lot…a CD of the world's best-loved Christmas carols.

Earth's Canopy

David Milarch

DEATH WAS NEAR; MY BODY shutting down. I lay limp in my bed at home, barely aware of my wife, Kerry, and my mother at my side. All I felt was sadness. And regret. What a waste. I was an alcoholic, too often an embarrassment to Kerry and our two sons, Jared and Jake. I didn't want my kids to see me like this.

Too late, I'd tried to get sober—cold turkey, here in my bed. But my liver and kidneys couldn't take the sudden withdrawal. I could barely breathe, my lungs filling with fluid. A friend took me to the emergency room, where they gave me a blood transfusion, but the doctor's face was grim. "We need to put you on dialysis," the doctor said. "That will give you time to say good-bye to your family." I'd come home a day ago. I was still alive. Barely.

Forty-one years. What had I accomplished? I was proud of the boys. Jared was twelve and Jake was ten, my helpers on our family tree farm. I'd tried to encourage them, told them never to give up on their dreams. But Kerry was really the one who'd seen to their upbringing. The farm, 150 acres in northern Michigan, was my other passion. We grew shade trees: maples, locusts, birch. *Did my life even matter?*

Suddenly I felt a hard pulse in my chest, like a thud. I floated from the bed toward the ceiling. I looked down. My body lay in the bed lifeless. I looked awful, bloated, my skin yellow and gray. Like I'd washed up on a beach. *Is this it?* I thought. *My time on earth over?*

I felt a touch, gentle, yet firm, on my right arm. I turned to see a beautiful female in a radiant white gown. There was a fragrance, sweeter than any flower. I breathed it deep into my lungs. "We know you're scared," she said. "But we're here to help."

"Who are you?" I asked.

"We're here to help you," she repeated. To my left there was another female, nearly identical to the first, holding my other arm. *Angels?* I wondered. *What do they want from me?*

We left the confines of the house and entered a tunnel of light. The walls were a brilliant white, except for the glow of a thin pink and blue helix running through it. Then we shot off, like we were on the tip of a missile. It scared the starch out of me. But it was only for a few seconds. I stepped out onto a vista. Below me a white, sandy beach leading to a vast body of water. In the distance a gleaming metropolis, lit by a prism of light, like a sunrise. I felt a comfort I'd never dreamed possible. Love. Unconditional love. It seemed to flow all around me, like waves caressing me. My sadness, my sense of failure left me. I wanted to stay here forever.

Dozens of light beings, radiant, glowing personages walked toward me on top of the water. They didn't have wings. They wore white gowns but the light, shimmering around each of them, was golden.

In the midst of them was another angel, a towering presence. He looked to be at least ten feet tall. He was clearly leading the others. Under a dark blue cape he wore a translucent gown of lighter blue.

I heard a booming sound, like thunder. It was the lead angel. "You can't stay. You must go back."

"But…" I started.

You have work to do," he said. *Work? What kind of work?* I didn't want to leave. But before I could get another word out I was hurtling through the white tunnel with the first two angels back to my bedroom. I lowered into my body, and then they were gone. But what was the work I was supposed to do? "Wait! Wait!" I shouted, suddenly sitting upright.

"David, what's wrong?" Kerry said, taking my hand.

It took a moment for me to know where I was. "It's nothing," I said. "But I know I'm going to get better. There were angels."

Kerry squeezed my hand. "Don't talk," she said. "You're so weak."

Day by day, week by week, my body healed. It wasn't easy. But every morning and night, I saw a small white glow near the ceiling. I lived for those moments, an assurance that God was still with me. *What is the work He wants from me?* I wondered. It made me nervous, not knowing. *What if I can't do it?*

But there was no further instruction. By fall I was strong enough to get out of bed. One day, with halting steps, I went out to the porch and sat in a lawn chair. Everything seemed more alive than I remembered it, the chickadees, jays, and finches singing so joyfully from their perches in the trees. I could almost sense what they were feeling—there was gladness and celebration, an energy about them, but also an unease—something not right in their world. It was amazing, like I was getting a glimpse behind a magical curtain. Could this be what God meant for me? To be more in tune with nature? I could do that. It was kind of nice actually.

But that wasn't the only change. I had no interest in alcohol. I got misty-eyed just sitting outside with the birds, working next to our sons on the farm, eating one of Kerry's home-cooked meals. I had a tenderness and compassion I'd never felt before. I couldn't understand it. Why was this happening to me?

Then one winter night I awoke just after one in the morning, surprised to find the bedroom lit by the warm glow that had given me such comfort. The light grew brighter and brighter until it was blinding. I covered my eyes with my hands, but it barely made a difference. Kerry was sound asleep by my side. "Okay, I'm listening," I said. "Just tell me what I need to do."

A soft, warm female voice said, "Get a pad and pen and go to the living room."

I rose out of bed, found a legal pad and a pen and sat nervously on the edge of my leather chair. But the voice was gone. My eyes grew heavy. I woke with a start and looked at the clock. 5:55 A.M. *But what about…?* I looked down at the pad in my lap. Page after page was filled with a detailed, formal outline. I stared in wonder at the words: *Dying trees. Champion species. Cloning. Reforesting.* It was my handwriting, but nothing I'd ever even thought about. I had no memory of taking any of it down.

My heart raced as I read through what I'd written. The earth's trees and forests were getting sicker, weakened by pollution, drought, disease, and bugs. I was to clone the biggest, strongest, hardiest trees—trees that had lived hundreds, even thousands of years—so the world could one day be restored to its natural order by the giants of the forest. I felt like Noah, a simple man told to become a shipbuilder and a zookeeper and…There had to have been a mistake. I wasn't a scientist. I didn't know the first thing about cloning or the environment. Where to even begin?

I needed help, a second opinion. I went to Jared's room and shook him awake. "I need you to read this and tell me what you think," I said.

Jared's eyes opened wide as he read. "Dad, this is amazing," he said. "Can I help? We need to do this."

"You really think we can?" I asked.

"Why not?" he said. "You're always saying nothing's impossible."

That summer, nearly a year after the angels first visited me, Jared and I collected our first DNA from a sugar maple, after learning the technique from researchers in Oregon. Seventeen years later, my original outline became a reality. It's grown from my family and me into a nonprofit with nearly a dozen employees and volunteers, the Archangel Ancient Tree Archive. We've taken DNA from more than sixty of the most magnificent trees on the planet—coast redwoods, giant sequoias, bristlecone pine thousands of years old, willow, and yew—enough to create thousands of trees. We've been helped by angels—both heavenly and earthly—every step of the way. We're all called to help the earth. You don't have to be a scientist. You only have to listen to the angel beside you.

Brush with a Blizzard

Winston Elliott

UP HERE ON THE NORTHERN Peninsula of Newfoundland, February blizzards come up right quick, and when they do, watch out. Snow blows in heaps from the northeast, pack ice piles up, and you can't see five feet in front of you. A man can lose his way just walking to a neighbor's house. It's weather you don't want to get lost in.

I should know. I had my own brush with a blizzard when I was just twenty-five. It happened on a chilly February Saturday here in Raleigh, where I've lived all my life. Raleigh's a tiny fishing town at the very tip-top of Newfoundland. The town's on a bay. Across the bay is Burnt Cape, a three-mile-long spit of rock joined to the mainland by a skinny isthmus. No one really lives on Burnt Cape. It's mostly limestone barrens and stands of stunted evergreen trees with gnarled roots called Tuckamores. Most of the cape is ringed by cliffs, some of them more than two hundred feet high.

That day I was home with my parents when my Uncle Gersh asked me to go to Ern Taylor's place at the south end of Raleigh, near the Burnt Cape isthmus, to pick up the key to the church. Gersh was the church caretaker, and Ern was a friend of his. I needed the key to open the church the next morning. Every Sunday I rang the bell to call the town to services.

It was a beautiful day, the sky clear, the air crisp and still. The temperature was around freezing, but I didn't mind. As a salmon fisherman I'd been out in all kinds of nasty weather. I pulled on my fishing boots, my coat, a wool cap I'd knit myself and worsted mittens. I'm tall, six feet four in my stockings, and my coat didn't quite fit—left a big gap between the bottoms of my sleeves and the tops of my mittens. Ern's was only a five-minute snowmobile ride away, so I thought nothing of it. On the way, I stopped at my friend Willie's for a few games of cards.

Willie was just dealing a hand of Five Hundreds when I looked out the window and saw thick snow falling. *Uh-oh.* Snow coming that fast meant only one thing: a blizzard. "Better get going," I said and hurried outside to start the snowmobile. I made it to Ern's, got the key and pointed the snowmobile home.

The blizzard howled out of the northeast, straight into my face. I jammed my cap low, pulled my coat collar close and gunned the snowmobile. I could hardly see, especially with my arm shielding my face. Soon I'd lost all sense of direction. The snow was a total whiteout.

I plowed on, praying I'd see something I recognized. Whatever road I was on bumped wildly. Something about the ground didn't look right. I peered closer. My heart leaped into my throat. It was solid ice under my snowmobile. Somehow I'd veered off the mainland and out into Pistolet Bay, onto the pack ice. If I went the wrong way I could end up driving off the ice and into the water. I had to get back to land. I made my best guess as to the right direction and gunned the snowmobile.

I bounced along in a howling world of white. The snowmobile groaned and wedged itself under a chunk of ice. I tried to back out, but the engine died. I peered at the fuel gauge. Empty. I listened. For some reason, the wind seemed to have died down here. Above, looming out of the drifts, I saw an immense dark shape. I was terrified until I realized the shape must be one of the cliffs of Burnt Cape. I'd chosen the right direction. I'd reached land.

I made my way to the cliff and looked up. The face was rocky and pitted. The skin between my mittens and coat was raw. I flexed my fingers. They moved—a little. I took a breath and began climbing. Fortunately here in the shelter of the cliff, the wind hardly blew. I climbed in silence, forcing my aching hands to reach from rock to rock. Finally I saw white above and all of a sudden, the wind returned with a vengeance. I hauled myself over the lip of the cliff and collapsed on a lichen-covered rock.

The blizzard raged around me. If I didn't get up I might lie there forever. I staggered to my feet and walked toward what I thought looked like a stand of trees. It was Tuckamores. I skirted alongside the windblown shapes, remembering that Tuckamores grow more numerous as you move south along the cape, closer to Raleigh.

The going was rough. Snow banked up around the roots and I kept plunging into drifts, terrified each time I'd tangle my feet in those roots. But I had no choice. If I strayed from the trees I could fall down the cliff.

Suddenly I spotted lights ahead. *Raleigh!* Hope flared in my heart but just as quickly died. The ground sloped down as it neared the isthmus, and I lost sight of the lights. I walked and walked, trying to rub life into my frozen hands and wrists.

At last a building appeared. I recognized Lewis Evans' fishing shed. I was at the very southern end of Raleigh, near the Anglican cemetery. For some reason I thought about Lewis's sister, Sadie, who'd died just a year before and was buried in the cemetery. She'd been a spinster, much beloved in town for her helpfulness.

I struck out into the storm again, thinking I knew my way. The wind seemed to slacken a little and every now and then I thought I saw shapes of buildings. But everything looked so different. I rubbed my eyes to see better, and tiny icicles fell from my eyebrows and beard.

A voice cried out, "You're going the wrong way! Follow the light!"

I looked around wildly but saw nothing. A human form seemed to retreat into the snow—but now it was gone. Maybe I was just seeing things. I was in the cemetery. Once again I'd taken a wrong turn. If I kept going this way I'd walk right back out onto the bay.

I retraced my steps until I saw a light. It was my friend Elijah Taylor's house. I burst through his door. Elijah's parents, Eve and Harve, took one look at me and set to work removing my coat, hat and mittens. Eve put a cup of hot tea in my hands, and I croaked out the most heartfelt thank-you I had ever uttered.

The next morning I was at church at seven pulling the bell rope. With every peal I thanked God from the bottom of my heart. I still don't know whose voice I heard out there in the howling storm. But perhaps it doesn't matter. There will always be storms in this life. What's important to remember is that God will always see us through them.

The Dream

Sharon Crisafulli

"GOOD NIGHT, JASON." I LEANED down and gently kissed my eight-year-old son's forehead as he snuggled under his comforter. He was wearing his favorite baseball pajamas. His hair, always a little too long, fanned out over the pillow. His eyes were already closed when I turned to leave. But as I was pulling the door shut, he called to me.

"Mom? I just had a dream."

I returned to Jason's bedside. "Honey, you haven't even been to sleep yet. How could you have had a dream?"

"I don't know, Mom. It just came to me right after I said my prayers." His brown eyes held a serious expression. "I was in school, at my desk," he said in a strange, matter-of-fact tone. "All of a sudden, I fell over onto the floor. People were staring at me. I was dead."

I sat with Jason until he fell asleep. His "dream" was disturbing; it seemed more than just a child's imagination.

Several times in my life I'd had similar experiences. I remember suddenly knowing my grandmother would die. Though she appeared to be perfectly healthy, she left us three days later. And I remember being certain a seemingly happy couple were having deep marital difficulties. I don't know how I knew; I just knew. Outwardly, they were the picture of marital bliss. A year later they admitted they had been near divorce at the time.

I went to bed wondering what Jason's dream was all about. Was it some kind of warning?

By the following week, however, the incident had been pushed to the back of my mind. Our home in Merritt Island, Florida, was a busy place, and I had plenty of other things to think about. Jason's school activities and caring for Nicole, his lively three-year-old sister, for example.

Then one night a week later, I sat up abruptly in bed, wide-awake. It was after midnight, and Jack, my husband, was sleeping soundly. For a moment I thought it was he who had woken me. But before I could give it another thought, I was overwhelmed with the need to pray—to pray for Jason.

As I eased out of bed, I felt tears streaming down my face. I crept into his room and gathered him into my arms. I cradled his warm body against mine as I prayed. I rocked him as I had when he was a baby. Jason slept soundly through it all.

Then it was over. The need to pray ended as suddenly as it had begun.

The next night it happened again—the sudden need to pray for Jason. And again the night after that.

There was a time in my life when I would have felt silly praying the way I did. There was a time when I would have told no one. There was a time when I would have been afraid.

But now I knew it was time to pray, and so I prayed.

By the third morning, my midnight prayers were becoming as predictable as the other routines of my life. As usual, I spent the few minutes before the children woke sipping coffee and savoring the quiet.

Nicole was usually the first to rise. But this morning she was still snoozing even after Jason was up and dressed for school.

It was gloomy and overcast. As I looked out the window, I was seized by a sense of sadness. Even as I made Jason's breakfast, my heart grew heavier by the moment.

I walked Jason to the end of our driveway. Right on time and with a whoosh of air brakes, the school bus pulled to a stop across the street, its red lights flashing.

Jason and I both looked up and down the busy highway. I gave him a quick kiss and he was on his way.

He never made it to the bus. His left foot had barely touched the pavement when a speeding station wagon came from nowhere and slammed into Jason, hurling his body fifteen feet into the air. He came down hard, headfirst.

It all happened so fast. Now, there he was, lying in the middle of the highway.

I fell to my knees beside him. His eyes were rolled back. His tongue was swollen and protruding. In a matter of seconds his right leg had swelled, straining the fabric of his jeans. His left arm was bent at a grotesque angle. I leaned close to his face and realized he wasn't breathing.

"No," I whispered. Then I lifted my head and screamed, "No, no, Lord, You can't let him die!"

A crowd gathered. They were all staring, horror-struck.

"Somebody call an ambulance!" I was amazed at the sudden control in my voice. "And get my husband, he's working in the orange grove down the road."

I bent over Jason and prayed out loud, "Dear God, I know You've raised people from the dead. Please raise up my son!"

I don't know how many people were in the crowd of onlookers, yet in their midst I suddenly felt a distinct presence. I glanced up and found myself looking straight into the eyes of a bearded man standing a few feet away. He had reddish-brown hair and stood relaxed with both hands in his pockets. Though it was only a second or two, it seemed like an eternity before he spoke in a surprisingly soft voice: "I have oxygen in my car."

Moments later the man knelt beside me and gently placed the mask over Jason's face. Almost instantly, Jason gasped and drew a long breath. Weeping with relief, I leaned over and whispered into his ear, "It's okay, son, just think about Jesus. You're going to be okay."

But when I turned to thank the mysterious stranger, he was gone. And although the road was jammed in both directions, no one saw him leave.

Jason was in the hospital for months. His thigh and arm were broken. He had a severe concussion. But amazingly, there was no permanent damage.

Now, ten years later, I still shudder when I think about what might have happened if I had not heeded those urges to pray, and pray hard. You see, I know that the bearded man who saved Jason's life wasn't just some passing motorist. He was part of something bigger. Something that involved Jason's dream. Something that required my waking three nights in a row to pray for Jason.

That mysterious man was part of a heaven-directed rescue, and he was there in answer to my prayers.

"Never Skate Alone"

Mike Marinaro

MANY WEEKENDS I GET UP before dawn and head to my favorite fishing hole, a wooded lake near my home in North Carolina. It's not just catching fish I like. It's the quiet. The time to think. The lake reminds me of the Oil Mill Pond in Danbury, Connecticut, where I used to fish and skate when I was a kid. I've often puzzled over something that happened to me there one winter when I was eight. I understood it then, or thought I did. But over the years I began to wonder if my explanation was nothing more than a kid's imagination. It involved an angel, after all, which isn't an everyday occurrence. And, truth be told, I haven't seen an angel since.

So, while I fish in my favorite fishing hole, I think. I've been over and over it a hundred times.

The Oil Mill Pond was near our house, and it was fun year-round. In winter, it was the greatest ice-skating place in the world—as long as you stayed a safe distance from the waterfall that descended from the mill dam to the rocks below.

One afternoon all I wanted to do was go skating. I'd been waiting for weeks until the water was frozen solid. Mom had one rule: "Never ice-skate alone." But that afternoon I couldn't wait any longer. So I hid my skates under my coat and ran to the pond.

At last! I thought. I sat on the bank and laced up my skates. Several people skated near the shore, and some kids were playing hockey. I'm not really alone, I decided.

Snow whisked across the glassy surface of the pond as I stepped onto the ice. I picked up speed, then twirled around, making figure eights. In some spots I could see how thick the ice was, with cracks and bubbles under the surface. At the far end of the pond the sunlight glistened in the waterfall. The ice stayed thin there because of the constantly flowing water.

I raced back and forth, and then spun in circles. The hockey game had attracted noisy spectators, so I skated in the other direction. Eventually the sounds of the cheering crowd faded away. All I could hear was the scraping of my skates cutting into the ice.

Another noise sent shivers down my spine. *Crack!* I looked up. I hadn't been paying attention. I had skated too close to the dam! The ice was cracking beneath me. It gave way. Freezing water covered my body, and I sank like a rock to the bottom of the pond. All I could think of was Mom. I hadn't done what she'd told me. For a few seconds I could see the circle of broken ice with the sun shining through. But as I sank deeper the circle became smaller, and the sun faded. Then everything was pitch-black. My feet hit the muddy bottom of the pond. *Swim to the top!* But my body was numb from cold. My gloves were soaked. I could hardly move my fingers. My lungs were about to burst. I had to breathe.

Just when I thought I wouldn't last another second, I felt a tap on my shoulder. "Don't try to swim, Mike," someone said. "If you do you'll lose your way." I swung my head around. I couldn't see anybody. But I heard the voice again: "Push your feet into the bottom, and you'll shoot straight up to the surface."

I did as I was told. I pushed myself upward with all my might. Everything was blackness. How would I find the hole in the ice? "Trust me," the voice said. Then a flash of bright light blinded me. I broke through to the surface of the pond, gasping for air. I thrashed around in the water, and then I felt myself being lifted, helped onto the ice by someone I couldn't see. I crawled to the shore and lay down, exhausted. The next thing I knew, people were standing around me, covering me with coats. Everything got blurry, and when I awoke, I was home in my own bed. Mom sat next to me, holding my hand. "Nobody saw me fall through the ice," I said. "Nobody was there to pull me out of the water. An angel came to my rescue."

Mom smiled. "I just thank God you're safe," she said. "Whatever happened, it was God's doing."

I've fished and fished, and I've thought and I've thought. For a long time I thought I'd come up with a more realistic explanation, if I just thought about it enough. Well, I've thought about it all I can, and I know the answer after all these years.

Mom was right.

Special Order

Lorraine Newkirk

BEING A SCHOOL COUNSELOR FOR junior high students in Minnesota was so rewarding that I felt my paycheck was a bonus. I loved every one of those kids—but, I wanted a child of my own.

I taught English for eight years and then went back for my master's degree in school counseling. That's when I met David. We married, but delayed starting a family until after we both had earned our master's degrees. Now, those degrees in hand, I was forty-five, and we were ready to have a child.

"You're too old to have a baby," my doctor said. "You should be pushing a golf cart around, not a baby carriage. Besides, that one kidney is not functioning efficiently. It would cause more kidney problems if you got pregnant."

That night David and I sat sadly and silently over our spaghetti. David said, "We can always adopt." But I wanted our own baby. My insides felt the empty loss of a lifelong dream.

I was also concerned about what my parents would say. I had always been a disappointment to them. I wasn't cute and petite like my cousins. At five feet ten inches tall by eighth grade, I was skinny, gangly, and wore glasses. My grandmother called me "Moose."

Mom said I would never find a husband. But I had found a great husband. David is intelligent, six feet two inches tall, and likes my grit and the fact that I can discuss philosophical issues with him. I had done well finding a good husband. But, I wanted my parents to see that I could have a beautiful baby too.

It took a few weeks to adjust to the bitter reality that I'd never hold my own baby in my arms. I didn't tell my parents. Finally, after much discussion, David and I applied for adoption.

We underwent all the background checks and home investigations while our excitement of having a baby grew. "Because of the age ratio between child and parent, you are too old to adopt an infant," the social worker told us. "But, you qualify to adopt an older child."

David and I walked out in a daze. Do we want an older child? My childless arms felt empty, heavy, old, guilty. I had failed again.

I began working toward a degree in education administration. I became the Sunday school superintendent at church. We haunted flea markets, searching for Red Wing pottery. David created the Red Wing Collector's Society and started a newsletter. We kept ourselves too busy to think about adopting a baby.

I eventually decided I didn't want a degree in education administration. As assistant principal, I would be the heavy hand of discipline. I wanted to be the soft glove to handle teenagers' issues. That fulfilled me in a special way. But, I still needed to be a mother. We decided to go ahead with adoption. We would love whichever child God chose to give us.

The next step in the adoption process was my physical exam. The examination revealed an almost unbelievable surprise. I was pregnant!

David and I were thrilled. The only pall over our excitement was the doctor's words; "You will have an arduous delivery at your age." I was almost forty-nine.

I walked around in wonder for weeks. God was clearly at work here. In August, my doctor ordered an amniocentesis test. "At your age the chances of having a Down syndrome baby, or a baby with spina bifida, increases greatly," he said. Whatever the test revealed, I would not abort this baby. This child was a precious gift from God.

During our wait for the results of the test, I worried that I might lose the baby. One in every two hundred amniocentesis tests resulted in miscarriage. The call finally came. "You have a normal female fetus."

I wept with joy.

Shortly after Christmas I developed pre-eclampsia, a condition that stresses the fetus and puts the mother at risk. The doctor ordered bed rest.

Every three days I had a blood test. Each test revealed more stress on the baby. I had to undergo another amniocentesis test to determine whether the baby's lungs were sufficiently developed for birth. I came home and went to bed with cramps and more worries about whether her lungs were developed enough and whether she would be born normal.

I lay in bed and looked out at the blustery, snowy day that made me even more fretful. I tossed and turned, urging sleep to come as an escape from my worries when a soothing voice said, *Don't worry, Lorraine. Everything will be all right.*

I was alone in the house with no radio or television on. It could only be the voice of an angel sent by God. I lay there in awe. I had heard that voice distinctly. My anxiety began to melt away like a patch of ice in a warm ray of sunshine. I began to envision our daughter. I wanted her to be spectacular. "Lord, give me a beautiful girl with red hair and green eyes," I whispered.

My great-grandfather had red hair, but no one else in the family, or David's family, had red hair and green eyes. Could my baby really have red hair and green eyes? No matter what this baby looked like, we would love her. But, wouldn't it be wonderful if she is beautiful?

On January 19, the doctor performed a C-section and delivered nine-pound-three-ounce Emilie Lynn Newkirk. She had spiky red hair and blue eyes. Three months later, her eyes turned green.

She was spectacular!

Mom died without ever having acknowledged that Emilie was a beautiful baby. But it didn't matter anymore. God loved me enough to give me a wonderful husband and a healthy, normal daughter, made to my own specifications.

I began to trust Him and call upon Him to comfort me when I needed comfort, to guide me when I wasn't certain which way to go, and to sustain me when I was unsure of myself.

And because of God's love, I finally learned to love myself.

Nothing to Hide

Deb Sistare

I WAS FIFTEEN WHEN MY dad died, and Mom took our family to live with Grandma and Grandpa. They were a perfect pair of opposites. She was short and plump; he was tall and skinny. She had a head full of wild white hair; he had a thin band of fuzz from ear to ear. She was always in high gear; he walked with an easy shuffle. Grandma went to church on Sundays; Grandpa didn't. "Why doesn't Grandpa go with us?" I finally asked my mother one Sunday while we were getting ready.

"He just doesn't," Mom said. "And you shouldn't ask such personal questions of people. It's just not polite." I hadn't meant to be hurtful. I loved Grandpa. After school I'd stop off at his barbershop and watch him cut hair in his careful, deliberate way. On warm summer evenings we'd sit under the pecan tree, and Grandpa would teach me life lessons. "If you borrow money and say you'll pay it back Friday morning, then do it," he said. "Even if you have to borrow it again on Friday night." Some nights, when Grandpa fell asleep in his old lounge chair, I'd put on red lipstick and kiss him on his bald head. When he woke up and came into the kitchen, Grandma would burst out laughing.

"What's so funny?" Grandpa would ask, two red lips standing out on his shiny head. Then he'd see me struggling to keep a straight face and go to the mirror, knowing I'd gotten him again.

Much as I became Grandpa's shadow, though, some things remained a mystery. Like why did Grandpa smell of cherry pipe tobacco during the week and on the weekends like whiskey? Plus, I'd seen his name on the church roll. Why had he stopped going?

One weekend I found Grandma frantically pulling towels out of the closet in the bathroom. "Did you lose something?" I asked. Grandma shook her head and stuffed a few more towels under her arm. "There it is," she said, sounding relieved. She held an unmarked bottle of amber liquid I knew was whiskey. As I watched, Grandma poured a trickle down the drain of the chipped porcelain sink. "If I empty it he'll just buy another bottle," she explained as she added water. "So I dilute it a little at a time. By tomorrow he'll be sober enough to go to work." Grandma put the bottle back in the closet. "I can't let him lose the barbershop." Without asking any questions, I handed her the towels, one by one, until everything was back in its place.

I watched Grandpa closely that week, but didn't notice anything unusual until Friday night. I smelled whiskey on him. When we got back from church on Sunday afternoon he was dozing in his easy chair. *He doesn't look drunk*, I thought. But when he got up and walked past me, eyes downcast, he didn't smile. His feet dragged like lead weights across the floor and into the bathroom.

I went to find my mother. She was reading in her bedroom. "What is it, Deb?" Mom asked. I hesitated.

"Is Grandpa okay?" I managed finally.

"Sure," Mom said, her tone clipped. "He's just tired. He worked hard all week." She went back to her book. Grandpa's just tired, I repeated to myself. Then I heard Grandma wrestling with the towels in the bathroom closet and went to help her. She stacked them in my outstretched arms. Grandpa must have been ashamed of his drinking, I figured, and that's why he tried to hide it from Grandma. Maybe that's why he doesn't go to church anymore. He wants to hide from God. Like the week before, Grandma stuck the bottle under the faucet without a word.

After a while, our Sunday routine seemed almost normal. Almost. Grandpa remained the same loving man, and he continued to be "tired" on the weekends. I grew up and moved out on my own, but I still visited my family regularly.

When I was thirty, Grandpa was diagnosed with terminal cancer. I spent a lot of time sitting beside his bed, talking to him. The whiskey bottle was never far away now. *He's too sick to hide it anymore*, I thought one night as I watched him sleep. Grandpa had spent too much of his life trying to keep his problem from us and from God. The worst part was that we had helped him do it.

"You should have asked God for help," I whispered to Grandpa, kissing his bald head. "We all should have."

Then I had an awful thought: If Grandpa's secret had kept him from church, could it keep him out of heaven as well? *Please, God, forgive us all. And take my grandpa into heaven.*

After Grandpa died, the thought continued to haunt me. One night I had a strange dream. Grandpa was standing at the bottom of a steep, pearl-white staircase that reached way into the clouds. He gazed up at a huge angel, who held out a satiny, emerald-colored robe, open and waiting, it seemed, for Grandpa himself. When Grandpa headed up the stairs, he wasn't shuffling. At the top of the stairs, the angel helped Grandpa into the robe and tied the sash so the rich folds of material fell around him. Then the angel took Grandpa's hand, and together they disappeared into the clouds.

The picture of Grandpa wrapped in that shiny emerald-green robe was fresh in my mind when I met Grandma for lunch the next day.

Grandma was adjusting slowly to life without Grandpa. "I miss him terribly," she admitted. "He was a good man. Even though he had a drinking problem."

I couldn't believe she had said it openly. "Yes," I said, "he did have a drinking problem." It was a relief to admit it out loud. But Grandma looked frightened.

"He didn't go to church," she said. "I don't know if he asked God's forgiveness. I'm so afraid he didn't go to heaven!"

I wrapped my arms around Grandma, feeling closer to her than I ever had in all the years I'd lived in her house. The secret that had always stood between us was gone. "Last night I dreamed about Grandpa," I said. Grandma sat very still and listened. When I got to the part where Grandpa slipped into the green robe, her eyes filled with tears. "He made it, Deb," she said. "He really made it."

"But, Grandma, it was just a dream."

Grandma shook her head. "Let me tell you something," she said. An expression came over her face that I'd never seen before. "Something we never told anybody else. One Sunday at church when we were first married, your grandpa saw an angel standing right on the altar. He said that angel was at least ten feet tall, standing right behind the preacher and smiling down at him during the service. And your grandpa said that angel was wearing the most beautiful green robe—'a robe that glistened like emeralds' were the words he used. 'When I get to heaven,' he said, 'I want a green robe just like the one that angel was wearing.' What else could that dream be but a sign from God that Grandpa is with Him?"

What else, indeed. God sees our weaknesses, and he loves us despite them. I believe he has an angel with an emerald-green robe waiting to welcome each of us, flaws and all.

Mr. Winters

Cookie Schnier

THE MOMENTS I TREASURED MOST during my time as a registered nurse at the hospice center were the initial walks down the dark corridor as I arrived early each morning. I would stop at each room and look in on the patients and family members as I made my way to the nurses' station to begin my day.

"How is everything with you this morning?" I would ask. One morning, Mr. Winters, who was to be discharged to his home in about a week, summoned me to come closer to his bed.

"I had a nightmare last night," he said to me. "I couldn't sleep. I dreamed I was in a place that had two tall iron fences, one in front of the other. Through the fences I could see many people on the other side that I knew had already died. They kept looking at me but didn't say a word. I managed to get the first gate open and when I got into that space between the first and second gate, the first gate closed behind me quickly and I was completely trapped. I had nothing, no food, no water, and nothing to keep me warm. I started calling and calling loudly for someone to help me, but none of those people could hear me. A strange-looking man appeared in front of me. He looked at me carefully and said, 'You need to do your paperwork first,' and then he simply went away. It's a terrible dream as I am completely trapped and I have no way to get out and no one to help me."

I sat down on the chair beside his bed and listened very carefully to him as he related this nightmare to me. He seemed relieved just to have someone to tell about it, and when he was finished he laid his head back onto his pillow, exhausted, and closed his eyes.

"We'll talk later, when you're rested," I said to him as I left the room to continue my morning rounds of visiting other patients.

Later in the morning I went back to visit Mr. Winters again, and we discussed the bad dream he had told me about earlier in the day. "Do you think this means something?" he asked me.

"Well, yes, I think it does," I said. "I believe you've been given a heads-up, if you will, that your time on earth is coming to a close and that you will have work to do to prepare yourself for your next life with your Creator."

"How am I supposed to do that?" he asked me. "I'm going home soon, you know. One day next week, for sure."

"Don't worry about next week," I said to him. "Right now you need to patch the holes that seem to be in your soul. God sends us messages in unlikely ways sometimes. This is one of those times. You need to pay attention now. You are blessed to be given this extra time and a chance to make everything right. This is a warning, and you need to get busy and make certain that everything is right between you and others and with your Creator. Open your heart to God, and together with Him start fixing what is unresolved in your life. Whatever is not resolved between you and your family or friends and whatever is not settled between you and God, work on that now. Ask Him to show you what you need to do and He'll help you, I promise." Mr. Winters remained quiet the whole time I was speaking, looking at me intently and taking in every word I said.

Every day for the rest of the week, Mr. Winters would sadly say to me each morning, "I had the nightmare again last night. It's terrible." Then he would repeat it exactly word for word, never changing any detail of it, as if it was etched in his mind and heart completely. Each day, I would prayerfully encourage him to ask

God to help him resolve everything that needed his attention, so that he could go home to Him in peace. It was evident to me that he was working on it in earnest, and so badly wanted it resolved.

One morning as I made my usual rounds, I stood in his doorway, trying to decide if he was asleep or awake. If he was sleeping, I did not want to disturb him, but when he sensed my presence, he turned to me and smiled. "Last night, the man came to me in my dream again. He said to me, 'Your paperwork is now finished, there is nothing left to be done.'"

With that, he peacefully rolled over, closed his eyes and fell asleep. He seemed relieved that his paperwork and all that it entailed had been completed, and now his heart could truly be at rest. During the next few days, Mr. Winters continued to be content and sleeping peacefully every time I stopped by to check on him. The day before Mr. Winters was to go home, he died in his sleep. His paperwork was completed, and he had now received his eternal reward, just as God wanted him to.

The Scriptures reflect many instances throughout history of God's messengers coming to earth to warn, to direct, and to enlighten His people. Joseph was warned by the angel to take Mary and Jesus into Egypt. Mary was told by the angel Gabriel that she was to be mother of Jesus, and Jacob's son Joseph knew, through a dream, that he would one day rule over his brothers. God enlightens our minds and hearts today, in the very same ways. He stays with us until the end of our lives, wanting us to come home to Him for all eternity.

Guardian Dear

Phyllis Swenson

JUST A FEW MORE MINUTES and school would be over for the day. I packed up my books and straightened my uniform, the same one worn by every girl at Blessed Sacrament Catholic School in St. Louis, Missouri. Finally the bell rang. "Bye, Sister," I called as I passed her at the door.

I followed the crowd down the hall, jostled and carried along to the front door. Once outside I ran down the steps and over to the church, where I waited for my father to pick me up. Inside it was quiet and peaceful. Statues of the angels looked down on me as I genuflected and made my way to the little chapel that was my favorite spot in the church. There hung the picture of two little children crossing a bridge. A beautiful blond angel watched over them, keeping them safe. I knew the world held more magic and mystery than people could ever imagine, but this guardian angel somehow made it all real to me. I recited the prayer Sister had taught us: "Angel of God, my guardian dear, to whom God's love commits me here. Ever this day, be at my side, to light and guard, to rule and guide. Amen."

The nuns said every child had a guardian angel, but sometimes I wondered if that really applied to girls like me. Girls who weren't white like the nuns at Blessed Sacrament and the little boy and girl in the picture. I was only in first grade back in 1959, but I knew black people and white people weren't considered equal by some. I heard my parents talk about it when they thought I wasn't listening. I'd even heard adults claim there were two separate heavens, one for white people and one for black people. God, they said, lived in the white heaven.

The angel in the painting looked so kind and loving, but she was looking after white children. Why would God bother sending an angel down from white heaven to look after me?

Because he's God, something in me said. I remembered all the things I'd been taught at church every Sunday with my family. "God is love," the priest had said just last week. Sister had said the same thing a hundred times. "God created all of us."

Why would God create me and not love me? I thought. In fact, why would God have created so many different people in the world who looked so many different ways if He only liked one kind of people? I looked up at the picture again. The joy and courage the angel always gave me came flooding back. Maybe I didn't have all the paintings and statues that white children had to prove that they had guardian angels, but I believed I had one all the same. Maybe black children had to have a little more faith. "Thank you, God, for my life and for my guardian angel," I said.

A car horn from outside broke me out of my reverie. I grabbed my books and dashed to the church door. When I got to the front steps, the strangest feeling came over me. It was like being engulfed in a presence, like a sacred mist. I'd never felt so peaceful or serene, even inside the little chapel.

I saw Dad behind the wheel of the car, but he was looking at something other than me. Even after I reached him he continued looking beyond me. I glanced back, but there was nothing there. I didn't want to disturb my peaceful feeling by asking a lot of questions. I got in. Neither of us said a word all the way home.

I was doing my homework in the living room when Dad said he wanted to talk. He sat down next to me and seemed to be struggling for words. He held my hand and took a deep breath. "When you came down the church steps today," he said, "I saw someone behind you. A tall, glowing lady with..." He hesitated. "A glowing bronze lady with huge wings!"

I gasped. My pencil rolled to the floor. "Wings?" I whispered.

"She was radiant," Dad continued, his voice going soft. "So radiant and beautiful I couldn't take my eyes off her. I could feel her incredible love for you pouring into me. I know I saw your guardian angel."

I didn't know what to say. Dad looked me right in the eye like what he was saying was the most important thing in the world. "You will always be protected by God and His angels," he said. "I want you to remember that always."

I flung myself into his arms. I did have my own guardian angel as beautiful as the one in the picture in the chapel. Never again would I wonder if God cared enough to send one just for me. My God, our God, who lives in one heaven for us all.

CHAPTER 5

Touched through Time

A Gift of Love

Sophy Burnham

As my friend Meg was driving to her niece's wedding, she realized her mother would have been eighty years old on this day, had she lived. Meg was filled with loss and grief. My friend is deeply spiritual, sensitive, intuitive. She knew it was silly, but she wished for a sign that the spirit of her mother was at the wedding, watching her grandchild's big day. I don't know if she prayed for it, but the longing certainly was there.

It was a huge wedding. There were four hundred people under a giant tent. There were tables and food and drink, music, dancing, and at midnight Meg found herself moving from her table to the far side of the tent, to watch the dancing from a different point of view.

Standing in the dark, she caught a glint of light in the grass at her feet. She reached down and picked up an exquisite sapphire and moonstone bracelet, and what was surprising was that it exactly matched the ring she had put on that evening for the wedding.

"It belongs to someone," she thought, clipping it on her wrist for safekeeping. "She'll call for it tomorrow, and then I can return it."

A little later the mother of the groom, who had been a friend of Meg's mother, saw her. "Oh, that's your mother's bracelet!" she exclaimed. "I've seen it on her many times."

How had the bracelet gotten there? How had Meg found it in the dark on the grass at midnight among a crowd of four hundred people?

"Of course you keep it," said her mother's friend. "I think she's just given it to you."

Visitor at Midnight

Pam Warford

I TOSSED AND TURNED IN bed next to my husband. I hadn't slept much in the two weeks since our third daughter, Katie, died in a drunk-driving accident. My days were a haze. Painful thoughts consumed me. *How could she have done it? Could I have stopped her?* Before the accident, I'd thought my second daughter was the one I had to worry about. She was going through a rough patch and her six-year-old daughter, Alana, stayed with me or her other grandmother most days. *Would life ever be all right again?* It seemed impossible.

My bedroom door creaked open. *Alana*, I thought, keeping my eyes shut. She often had bad dreams and came to our room just to make sure her grandfather and I were there. I could hear her gentle breathing. I'd learned if I pretended to be asleep, she'd go back to bed. I listened for retreating footsteps.

Instead, I felt Alana's soft cheek press against mine. "It's all all right," she whispered. "It's all all right."

A sweet surprise, a six-year-old's comfort. But it helped. I drifted off.

The next afternoon, Alana came by after school and joined me, my mom, and my sister in my living room. As we chatted, I mentioned Alana's visit the previous night.

"She told me, 'It's all all right,'" I said.

Alana spoke up. "No, I didn't!"

"You probably forgot, sweetie," I insisted. "It was late."

"But, Grandma, I wasn't here last night," she reminded me. "I was staying at my other grandma's house."

Love in the Lava

Joan Wester Anderson

GEORGIA LEA HORVATH AND HER husband, of North Bend, Washington, were grieving the loss of their twenty-six-year-old son, Scott. The three of them had planned to visit the big island of Hawaii in November, but as the departure date approached, neither wanted to go. One day, however, Georgia thought about it again. Maybe the trip would distract them for a while. They could invite her mother along too. And so they did.

The island was beautiful. One morning Georgia and her husband took a walk along the beach where black lava had hardened in the water. All around the Big Island, people leave names and messages made out of white stones on this lava, so they decided to leave a message for Scott. "*Aloha*, Scott," it read. (*Aloha* means "hello," "good-bye," and "love.") The couple took a picture of it and walked on.

"The next day we took my mom for a walk," Georgia recalled, "and when we reached that place, she spotted the message right away." Georgia thought it would have been washed away by the waves because it was right next to the ocean. Everyone was thrilled that the writing was still there.

On that day, the Horvaths had planned to take a twelve-hour drive around the entire island. But the night before, a fellow tourist suggested they avoid a certain area. "Don't bother to turn off at the south end of the island, to see the most southern tip of the United States," he cautioned them. "It isn't worth the drive on a dirt road, and nothing is there anyway." The couple agreed. This man certainly knew more than they did about tourist attractions.

They had completed the first part of their journey, and Georgia was driving when she saw the sign: Turn Here to See the Southern-Most Tip. "Remember," said her husband, "this is where that man said to go back."

"I remember," Georgia said, and started to turn. Then, at the last minute, she veered the other way, bouncing down the dirt road. "We're here," she said to her surprised husband. "Let's go as far as we can."

He shrugged. Up ahead he could see more black lava, just like the kind they had seen yesterday. Just then the path ahead separated, and Georgia had to turn left or right. "My hand seemed to turn toward the left," she said, "so this is where I went."

They drove to the edge of the lava and stopped. The area was completely deserted, just water splashing along the shore and, once again, lots of white stone messages all over from people who had visited. "We got out of the car and started to walk," Georgia said. "Then all three of us stopped. Ahead of us was a message written on a white stone: "Love U 2," it said. "Scott."

All three adults started to weep. "It was a message from Scott," Georgia said. "We know he didn't actually write it, but the fact that we almost didn't go to that area, and when we did stop, it was the right place … well, we were meant to see it." It made their trip and aided their healing. Scott was not gone, they knew, just enjoying a beautiful piece of heaven.

An Irish Christmas

Kathy Keeley Anderson

BAPA WOULDN'T WANT US TO be sad on Christmas. That's what I kept telling my children after my father, their "Bapa," died. But this was our first Christmas without our Irish Da, who loved any reason to celebrate—especially the holidays.

"Maybe we should do something to honor his memory," I suggested to my daughter, Catie. But what? "Bapa was so proud of being Irish," Catie said. "We could wrap a green ribbon around every present this year. He'd love making Christmas more Irish."

We bought rolls of green ribbon and tied up every package under the tree. Green was our color theme this year. And surely Bapa was smiling down on us from heaven.

Christmas Eve morning Catie went outside to admire the snow. "You have to come see this!" she called in to me.

Catie pointed to the highest tree in the yard. "Look!"

From the topmost branch, a shiny green ribbon fluttered and waved at us as if it had fallen from the sky. Perhaps it was a stray piece Bapa was using in his Irish Christmas up above.

On the Brink of Heaven

Bethany Withrow

ALL NIGHT THE POUNDING OF my heart kept me drifting in and out of sleep. Now, on a frosty December morning in 1994, I pulled myself from underneath the warm blankets with great difficulty. Every day, it seemed, I awakened more exhausted than the day before.

Eight years earlier, at seventeen, I had been diagnosed with lupus erythematosus, a degenerative systemic condition that produces a range of debilitating, sometimes mysterious symptoms, including arthritis. For months I had been battling a severe flare-up that had kept me prisoner in my house—except for stays in the hospital when I had a fever as high as 106 degrees. As a result of steroid drugs, I developed diabetes. Today I felt worse than I had in months.

Even breathing was painful. But something stranger was happening. When I touched my face, it felt unusual. I hobbled to the bathroom and sought my reflection in the mirror. Staring back at me was a face I hardly recognized. It was horribly swollen and my left eye drooped.

"Butch!" I called to my husband. He took one look at me and ran for the phone. "I'm calling the doctor."

Dr. Alexander told him to bring me right over. My husband had been by my side through many lupus crises, so to see him this unnerved scared me. I began to worry that I had suffered a stroke. Then in the living room, as I struggled with my coat, a flash of brown through the window caught my eye. There in our wooded yard stood a baby white-tailed deer all alone. *How strange he came this close*, I thought. Our gazes met and lingered, and I began to feel calm. I love animals. Suddenly, with a graceful little jump, he was gone. But a small measure of that calmness stayed with me.

We were almost out the door when my mom called from Wichita, Kansas, to check on me. I could tell how worried she was. When I was little, Mom used to say she asked God for a "hedge of angels" to protect her children. I reminded her to ask God to keep His angels close to me today.

Lupus is a disease of many guises, and Dr. Alexander couldn't determine what was wrong with me or how to treat it. He took X-rays and drew blood, then sent me home to rest. "Keep still and call me immediately if you get worse, Beth," he said. I knew he was trying to spare me another traumatic hospital stay. Unless my condition was life-threatening, I wanted to be at home.

In the car I studied Butch. I knew he hated leaving me to go in to work. He walked me inside the house and made sure I was comfortable on the couch. Then, as he leaned over to kiss me, I felt a tear fall on my brow. "Don't worry," I whispered. "I'm going to be all right."

But the symptoms worsened. I tossed and turned on the couch, my heart thundering. Late in the day, I finally tried calling Dr. Alexander but couldn't reach him. I was getting weaker. I talked to Mom again, and she said she and her friends at church were praying for me for all they were worth. After we hung up, Mom was so worried she called my father, who lives nearby. He came over to check on me and wasted no time getting me to the hospital.

By midnight I was once again in intensive care, hooked up to oxygen and a slew of beeping, blinking monitors. Butch had taken up his familiar position in a recliner by my bed, while doctors and nurses paraded in and out of my room. Eventually, around 3:30 in the morning, the traffic slowed. Butch nodded off while holding my hand, and I thought I was falling asleep too. Then I realized something altogether different was happening to me, something both wondrous and fantastic.

I drifted in a smoky grayness, not quite floating and not quite walking. I was free of all the medical equipment I had been tethered to moments before. I traveled down an extended passageway. It felt like being inside a telescope; in the dim distance I discerned a glow. With amazement I realized I was no longer in pain. I moved effortlessly toward a radiant, golden light. As I drew closer, I noticed a beautiful figure within the light, standing with outstretched arms. Indescribable peace flooded my senses; the feeling expanded the closer I came to the figure emanating from the light.

All at once I knew I was in the presence of the Son of God. Angels were everywhere, flying to and fro as they hastened to do the Lord's work, each encircled in its own golden bubble of light. Their flowing gowns were translucent and their features were serene, noble, and wise.

I was aware of Jesus communicating directly with me, though no words were uttered. His language flowed through me. He told me not to be afraid, that He wasn't ready for me yet, that I would be going back: *There are still things for you to do and songs for you to sing.* An overpowering sensation of being loved seized me. I felt a joy I had never felt before—the full experience of Christ's love for me.

Suddenly, as if a curtain had been drawn back, I found myself amidst breathtaking surroundings: magnificent mountains, rolling pastures, and singing brooks. I saw a distant red barn and I was happy because I knew this meant there were animals in heaven. I thought of the baby deer I had seen that morning and all the animals I loved.

I noticed a couple standing behind Jesus, and angels hovering and singing above them. I recognized my grandmother, who, before she died the previous year, had been doubled over with osteoporosis. Now she stood straight and tall, holding the hand of my granddaddy. He died long before I was born but I had seen many pictures of him. In his free hand he held a bowl.

I knew what it contained. Mama loved to tell about her daddy's prowess in the kitchen. Saturdays were special. That's when Granddaddy reveled in making his special chili, full of secret, savory ingredients. That bowl contained Granddaddy's Saturday-night chili, and far from seeming irrelevant or bizarre, this fantastic detail reassured me that my grandparents were happy, together again in their love, and that heaven was a place God has made for each of us.

Then Jesus was communicating with me again. "I have given you a special husband, and I have given him strength so he can care for you." I was always aware that Butch was unique; now the words of Jesus filled me with pride and gratitude.

He reminded me once more that there was much left for me to do; then I was zooming backward through the telescopic passageway as if time had been reversed. Almost instantly I was in my hospital bed again, reattached to the monitors and oxygen. But I was not disappointed. I was thankful and brimming with joy.

Immediately I wanted to tell Butch all about my amazing experience, but he was sleeping so peacefully, I did not have the heart to disturb him. I wondered why the monitors hadn't sounded an alarm while I was gone. My journey had seemed to last a long while. God's time, though, is different; what feels to us like hours may be only a blink of the eye in heaven.

For the first time since returning, I looked around the room, and there they were: angels, angels everywhere, flickering like candlelight, hovering protectively around us like a hedge—a hedge of angels.

No one sleeps late in the hospital. Soon the nurses and doctors were busy, and Butch woke up. I told him my experience, and he listened intently, stroking my hand, never doubting for a moment that what had happened to me was real.

All that day things looked markedly different, as if a bit of the light I had seen now touched and infused everyone and everything I encountered. I continued to sense the presence of heavenly beings in my room. Even Butch seemed to have an angelic glow about him.

The doctors were amazed to see that the swelling in my face had gone down and the position of my eye was back to normal. They continued running tests for the next few days, including an MRI. When they slipped me into the cylinder for that test, it was like being back in the heavenly passageway, and again I saw the angels. In the waiting room before the test, a frightened little boy was waiting his turn. I saw an angel hovering over him. I told him what I saw, and he became calm.

At last Dr. Alexander said I could go home. "All we know, Beth," he reported, "is that you suffered a major lupus flare-up, and now you're getting better. But you were very, very sick." Then, smiling, he said, "Don't scare me like that again."

I don't want to scare anybody because I know from my journey that there is nothing to fear when we are with God. He protects us and loves us at all times. Full awareness of that love is the greatest healer of all.

Nothing about life has been the same for me since I saw the angels. I no longer have to take insulin; my fever is gone; my heart beats normally. I still have lupus and I get sick, but it is not as bad or as terrifying as before. Now I have a continual sense of life's secret beauty.

I finally sat down and told Mom the whole story, and she cried tears of elation that her parents were happy with God, and that a hedge of angels protected her daughter.

Valentine's Day Gift

Jeanne Glasgow

VALENTINE'S DAY ALWAYS MADE ME pine for my husband, Jim, more than usual, and that was a lot. *I know he's waiting for me in heaven, Lord*, I thought, looking up at the sky. *And I'll get to see him again.* I tried to hold tight to that thought, but sometimes I wished I had a tangible reminder.

My son walked in and surprised me with a Valentine's Day gift—a dozen red, heart-shaped balloons. I stuttered a thank-you.

"They're not from me, Mom," he said. "I was sitting in the front yard when I saw them floating way up high. They were several blocks away, but I had the strangest feeling they were coming to our house."

"And they did?" I asked.

"They floated low enough to the ground that I could reach up and grab them. But they're not for me. I just know they're meant for you."

A tangible reminder blown right down from heaven to my front door. Jim would always be my valentine.

Confetti

Marion Holster

NOBODY LOVED LIFE MORE THAN Daddy. "I don't think it's possible to live long enough to do all the things I want to try," he once told me. Daddy sure came close: He'd been a rancher, a rodeo cowboy, a soldier in World War II, a salesman, a poet, a preacher, and a local radio and television personality. The Lord gave him ninety-one good years, and Daddy turned every one into a celebration.

"It doesn't seem right that the last event Daddy will go to is a funeral," I told my mother the morning of his burial.

"He would have much preferred a party," she said. "Streamers and confetti were more his style."

But without Daddy, we couldn't imagine having a party.

The memorial service opened with a hymn, "When We All Get to Heaven," and everyone in the church sang along: "What a day of rejoicing that will be."

The instant the song was finished a wind passed over Daddy's casket. The papers on the preacher's stand flew up into the air like an explosion of confetti. Mom and I looked at each other in happy surprise. Daddy wanted us to know he was in heaven. That was something to celebrate.

Heaven-sent

Tim Sherrill

IT HAD BEEN ONE YEAR, almost to the day, since my dad passed away. He was seventy-two years old, a former marine, a tough guy, but as kindhearted as they come. Dad was a bricklayer by trade, and he was dedicated. When he built something, he built it right, taking care of every last detail.

I began working with him in junior high, eventually becoming his partner, and later, his boss—even though it was in title only.

So I suppose it was fitting that a year after his death, on a rainy February morning, I was preparing to do the work Dad had taught me, helping my friend, Rick, build a huge patio onto his new home. The two of us were waiting for block and mortar supplies scheduled to be delivered just after noon. "Want to grab lunch real quick?" Rick asked.

I looked at my watch. Nearly eleven. We needed to be on site when the delivery arrived so we could oversee placement of the materials. Otherwise, we'd be breaking our backs if we had to move everything around ourselves through the mud. "Well, I guess we have some time," I said.

Turned out we didn't. We hurried back, but the supplies were already there. Probably all in the wrong place, I worried. Instead we found the blocks exactly where we wanted them. Even the sand and mortar mix were in the most conve-nient spots.

Grateful, we called up the delivery company. "Don't thank me," the delivery-man said. "An older gentleman told me what to do."

"Older gentleman?" I asked, puzzled.

"A tough old guy, built like a marine," the man said. He proceeded to describe my father, down to the last detail.

Angelic Escort

Donna Weaver

I WAS ON A BUSINESS trip when Dad passed away, finally losing his battle with kidney disease.

"Don't worry. I've already booked you a flight home," my husband, Mark, told me over the phone. "I'll be waiting at the airport to pick you up. I love you."

I cried the entire flight. Dad had always been so strong—he was a soldier in World War II—and seeing him so weak had been painful. *But not as painful as this.* Tears filled my eyes as I got off the plane. I could barely see. All I wanted was to be taken care of, to fall into Mark's comforting arms. But I felt lost and alone in the throng of travelers.

I asked a guardsman for help. "I just lost my father," I said between sniffles. "I'm supposed to meet my husband here, but I'm all turned around."

"I'll show you the way," he said softly. He looped my arm through his and led me out of the crowd past the security gates. I spotted Mark right away. "There he is!" The soldier escorted me over, and I wrapped my arms tight around Mark's waist. When I looked over my shoulder the soldier was gone. "What is it?" Mark asked.

"My escort, the soldier," I said. "Where did he go?"

Mark looked at me strangely. "There was no soldier with you, Donna. You walked over to me alone."

Batteries Not Included

Nan Closson

MERLE WAS ALWAYS COMING UP with ways to entertain our grandsons when they visited town. This time he put his hands on quite a contraption: a mechanical dog. He loaded the batteries, and we tested it before the boys arrived. The dog walked and barked and moved its head. Merle pressed a button to make its tail spin like a propeller. You couldn't help but laugh.

The boys played with the dog every single day, but nobody could get that tail to wag the way Merle could. I caught him fooling with the dog even after the boys had gone back home. "Merle!" I said. "You're a grown man!" Merle's hearty laugh made me think he'd live forever. But that wasn't to be. His health started to fail, and he died on an afternoon in March.

All of us struggled in the days after. One night I roamed the house, utterly joyless. *Lord, will I ever laugh again?* Suddenly I heard a whirring noise in the bedroom. I crept down the hall to the closet. Holding my breath, I opened the door.

Merle's little dog was spinning its tail a mile a minute. I burst out laughing. *Oh, Merle*, I thought. *Ever the entertainer.* I picked up the control box. The batteries weren't even inserted.

Scent from Above

Jacquelyn Buige Raco

MY GRANDMA BUIGE LIVED TWO blocks away when I was a little girl, and I loved visiting her. Her house was like a refuge. As soon as I stepped in and smelled that special smell—a mixture of her Tabu perfume, the Oil of Olay she smoothed on her face, and the fresh flowers she kept on her dining table, I felt safe and comforted.

Grandma Buige saw me through every step of growing up, and when she died one week after I graduated from college I knew nothing could ever replace her presence in my life. I missed her terribly, and wished she could have been there when I got married a few years later and then had two children of my own.

I really needed Grandma Buige when my little son, Griffin, didn't seem to be putting on weight. I arranged for him to see a specialist. During the week before the appointment I prayed every day—*Please, God, I want Griffin healthy*—but my anxiety only grew. Then one afternoon as I was putting Griffin down for a nap, I paused. There was a distinct fragrance in his room. Familiar somehow. Of course. I was sure. It was that mixture of Tabu perfume, Oil of Olay, and fresh flowers.

Where is that coming from? I wondered. It smells just like Grandma Buige's old house. Yet I couldn't find its source. Griffin's whole room smelled like Grandma Buige's. And only his room, nowhere else. Just like when I was a girl, I felt comforted and safe. From that point on, whenever I began to worry about Griffin, I would go to his room, where the smell of my grandma's house was all around.

Later that week the specialist confirmed that there was no need to worry. Griffin might grow more slowly than other children, but he was perfectly healthy. Relieved, I brought my baby home from the doctor's. When I put Griffin to bed that evening, I noticed the scent again, but only faintly. The next morning it was gone altogether. Grandma Buige's comforting fragrance had been there when I needed it, wafted in on the wings of an angel.

CHAPTER 6

Animal Angels

An Angel of a Dog

Lois Spoon

WHEN I FOUND A MARBLE-SIZE lump in my breast I tried to tell myself it was nothing. I was forty-two and had enjoyed good health my whole life. But deep down I knew better: My mother had died from breast cancer, which meant I was high risk.

Finally I summoned my courage and called the doctor. A mammogram and a biopsy confirmed my worst fear. The lump was malignant and doctors advised a radical double mastectomy. I agreed to have the surgery. And although all of my medical questions were answered and my husband, Robert, and son, Luke, gave me endless amounts of love and support, I kept a lot of my worries to myself. I wished for another woman to talk to. Someone who understood completely what I was going through. *Lord, help me through this. I feel like I'm on my own.*

Only days after the four-hour surgery I was released from the hospital, but I still seemed to spend more time with doctors and nurses and counselors than I did at home. I went to physical therapy every day, but rehabilitation was slow. Simple things such as rolling down a car window or opening a jar of peanut butter had become painstaking tasks.

Then at a follow-up visit with my oncologist I got even worse news. The cancer had spread far into my lymphatic system. "Frankly, Lois, we can't be optimistic about the prognosis," the doctor said, unable to cushion the blow. Even with chemotherapy, the odds of my surviving were small.

Back home I sank onto a chair and watched the rain through the window. I had never felt so completely alone.

I got up to draw the curtains when I noticed a Siberian husky trotting up the front walk as if he knew just where he was going. I'd never seen him in the neighborhood. I went over to the picture window. The dog cocked his head slightly and studied me. He came closer to the window and I saw he had one blue eye and one brown. For a few moments he stared at me, then went to sniff around the front yard.

Wait a minute, I said to myself. *Where did I just read about a missing husky?* I grabbed the previous day's paper from the coffee table and thumbed to the lost-and-found section in the classifieds. There it was—a description of a lost dog exactly like this one. I went to the phone and dialed the number listed. A woman answered. "I think your dog is in my yard," I told her.

"I can't believe it," she said. "Wolfy's been missing for weeks. Please give me your address. I'll be right over."

I hung up and went back to the window. How could I make sure the dog would stay until his owner came for him? Robert and Luke were out, and I couldn't restrain the big animal on my own. It would be hard to control him if I let him in. *He seems content just to sniff around outside*, I thought.

Sitting back down, I tried to keep an eye on the dog as he wandered around the yard. In about ten minutes a knock came at the door. "I'm Becky," the woman said. "Where's my Wolfy?"

"You don't see him in the yard?" I looked for myself. "Oh no! He was here just a second ago."

"I'll check around the neighborhood," she said. "He couldn't have gone far."

The woman returned about twenty minutes later. "Well, he's managed to disappear again," she said. "But I'm grateful you called me."

I felt awful for Becky. That, on top of my own problems, got me dabbing my eyes with a tissue.

"Are you okay?" Becky asked.

"Yes," I said. But she persisted. "You sure?" All of a sudden a gush of tears poured from my eyes. How could I let a stranger see me like this?

"Let's talk about it," Becky said, patting my arm. Something told me it was okay, and I invited her in. "My name's Lois," I said. We sat on the sofa, and I explained what was happening to me. She listened to every detail. When I finished she put her arms around me.

"Lois, I want to tell you something," she said. "Four years ago I had the exact same diagnosis and the exact same prognosis. Just like you I was given little hope for survival. But here I am. It can happen to you too," she said. "God will stand by you every step of the way—and so will I."

That day I gained immeasurable strength from Becky. I confided all my deepest fears to her, and it made me feel better when she said, "I know what you mean. That's how I felt too." She became a wonderful friend, always knowing just the right words to encourage me when I didn't think I could stand another round of chemo. Sad to say, though, she never did find Wolfy—God had other plans for him.

It's been six years since my surgery. I beat the odds. With Becky in my corner, I'm not surprised. I think it's safe to say that a dog only heaven could have sent wanted me to meet her.

Cardinal Calls

Dorothy Crawford

MORNING LIGHT FILTERED THROUGH THE curtains on the French window. My first thought of the day was of my husband, J.G. It had been the same every morning for the past couple of weeks since his death in January. We'd been married twenty-six years. I couldn't get used to the world without him. It was as if all the brightness had disappeared from my life.

J.G. was bright in so many ways. Bright smile, bright laugh—he even liked bright colors. Turning over in my bed, I could almost see him behind the wheel of a red pickup truck. As the owner of his own construction business, J.G. was in charge of choosing what vehicles they would drive. He knew exactly what color he wanted. "Are all your trucks red?" a new employee once asked him.

"Is there any other color?" J.G. said. Not as far as my husband was concerned.

Even illness wasn't enough to dull J.G.'s bright spirit. A stroke made it difficult for him to get around. At first he used a walker, but after a couple of falls he realized that was too risky. It was time to get something safer, like a motorized wheelchair.

J.G. and I went to a medical supply store to pick one out. "We have a wide selection," the man at the store said. "What are you looking for?"

"Anything in red?" J.G. asked.

"A red wheelchair?"

"Bright red," said J.G. "Like a cardinal's feathers."

I was sure he was going to be disappointed. Red trucks were easy enough to come by, but who paints wheelchairs to look like fire engines? The salesman disappeared into the back of the store and returned wheeling a chair in cherry red. "I'll take it," said J.G. without even bothering to try it out.

The salesman grinned and directed us to the cashier. "That was easy!"

Bright red, like a cardinal's feathers, I thought as I sat up in bed. J.G. made everything as bright as a cardinal's wings. Cardinals, of course, were J.G.'s favorite bird. We didn't see too many in Houston, where we lived during the week. But when we drove out here into the deep country on weekends we knew those red birds would be everywhere. J.G. had counted on it when he built this house. He'd made sure to include a big wooden deck surrounded by trees. Every evening the two of us sat outside, listening to the wind in the leaves and the call of the birds.

"I think there are even more cardinals around since I got my wheelchair," J.G. said to me one breezy evening after dinner. Some people wouldn't think of a wheelchair as cheerful, but people always smiled when they saw J.G. ride by in his. Maybe the birds felt the same way. Maybe they considered him one of them.

"They probably like the color as much as you do," I said.

J.G. turned toward the trees. "Miss-you! Miss-you!" he called, imitating one of their signature calls. He cocked his head and listened. I held my breath. A moment later, sure enough, came an answer from above us. *Miss-you! Miss-you!*

"Can you believe some of the men at work don't believe I can talk to cardinals?" J.G. said.

I'd been skeptical of J.G.'s claim myself until I'd witnessed one of their "conversations." The birds really did seem to respond to his imitations of their call.

What I wouldn't give to hear one of J.G.'s cardinal calls right now, I thought, looking into the gloom of my bedroom. Opening the curtains would let in the sunlight, I knew, but it wouldn't bring back the brightness I'd lost in my life. I was just about to lie back down and pull the covers over my head when something tapped hard on the window. What on earth?

The urgent tapping came again, even louder this time. I went to the window and pushed aside the curtain. Sunlight poured into the room. I blinked at the cross-piece on the window. Looking back at me from his perch there was a bright red cardinal. "Miss-you! Miss-you!" the cardinal called, cocking his plumed head to look into my face.

The room suddenly got brighter—and it wasn't the sunlight. Apparently J.G. was still talking with the cardinals—or the angels—and sent one to make sure I wasn't letting grief get the better of me. There was still plenty of brightness in the world, and this little red bird wasn't going to let me forget it.

The cardinal stayed close to the house all day. He peeped in at one window, then another, as if he were making sure I was okay. For the next few weeks he visited me every day.

J.G. is no longer with me in this world, but I can still find brightness in red pickups, cardinal songs, and the love of God Who made them all.

No Such Animal

Carter Allen

MY GIRLFRIEND DAWN AND I stayed out late into the night not long after New Year's Day. It was snowing heavily when we got into my car, and we decided to go only as far as my mother's house, about ten miles away. I drove slowly, the headlights of my compact boring white tunnels in the swirling flakes.

Around 1:30 AM, about a half hour after setting out, we turned onto Mom's road in a rural area near the northern Minnesota town of Walker. There were only a couple of dwellings on the two-mile stretch leading to her house, and Mom knew all the comings and goings in this quiet area.

By then the storm had become a raging blizzard. The windshield wipers groaned, protesting the mounting accumulation. Ghostly drifts shrouded the road and I tried to keep the wheel steady. I shifted into low gear and Dawn gasped. "Don't worry," I assured her. "We'll make it."

No sooner had I spoken than we hit a hidden dip. The car lurched sideways and I struggled to regain control as we shot into a ditch. "Hold on," I said. The wheels spun futilely when I pressed the accelerator. We were stuck.

"What now?" Dawn whispered.

"We'll have to shovel our way out as best we can," I said.

I reached onto the floor of the backseat. All I had was a snowbrush. Dawn and I got out. Squinting against the stinging crystals, she wielded the brush and I scooped the white powder with my hands, trying desperately to free up space around the tires. But as fast as we dug, the driving snow relentlessly filled in the gaps.

We looked at each other in desperation. The windchill must have been way below zero, with the gale shrieking off the flat fields bordering the road. Our tennis shoes, jeans, sweaters and jackets were no match for the cold. We climbed back into the car and started the engine to warm up. But in about fifteen minutes it died.

"Snow blocking the exhaust," I sighed. We sat quietly for a moment, the howling wind stealing through every possible crack. Thick frost built up on the windows.

Think, I told myself. Mom's house was still a good two miles away, too far to walk in this terrible storm.

"Remember that house about a half-mile back?" I asked Dawn. She nodded. "Maybe we can get help there."

"I can't think of any other way out," she said. "Let's go. It's worth a try."

Again we ventured into the blizzard, which had now become a whiteout, and plodded through knee-deep drifts toward the house. After some ten yards, I looked back. I couldn't see Dawn. I couldn't see more than five feet.

"Dawn!" I called. "Can you hear me?" Retracing my path, I found her. She looked dazed.

"Thought I was right behind you," she said. She wasn't going to make it. I led her back to the car, settled her in and took off running as fast as I could to the house.

Finally I stomped onto the dark stoop and pounded on the door. After a while a porch light blinked on and a man pulled open the inner door. I saw him pull the screen door shut.

"I'm sorry to wake you," I said, "but my car is stuck in a ditch, and my girlfriend and I are stranded."

"Can't help you," the man said, his face set, and he started to push the door closed. I could see that he was old and frightened, but I tried again. "Please, I just need to use your phone."

"Don't have one," he said. "And my car doesn't work. Like I said, I can't help you." He shut the door. The light went off.

What are we going to do? Tears froze on my face as I headed back to the car. My shoulders and back tense from bracing against the driving snow, I trudged on, feeling weaker with every step. Stumbling along, I was dimly aware of something following me. But I was so exhausted, so agonizingly cold, it was all I could do to put one foot in front of the other. I didn't have the strength even to turn around and investigate. *Too much effort*, I thought sluggishly. "God," I said, "only You can help us now." Then, my head swimming in blackness, I pitched forward into a drift. When I came to, a prickly, hairy form covered me like a blanket. *What...?* Some sort of a huge black dog had lain on top of me. "Good boy," I whispered, rubbing my hands in the stiff fur under his neck. *Is he wild?* I wondered. No pet would be out in this weather. I looked into his eyes. He seemed somehow to want to help me, almost as if he knew why we had crossed paths.

I pressed my face into his thick fur and breathed the air warmed by his body. The dog stood up.

What a magnificent animal, I thought. I had never seen a similar breed. Feeling new strength, I rose and headed for the car. I half expected the dog to continue on with me, but looking back I saw nothing; my dark rescuer had disappeared into the storm.

I found Dawn shivering. "I didn't have any luck at the house," I told her. "But on the way back, something incredible happened."

We huddled close in the backseat, and I began to describe my encounter with the mysterious black dog. "What was he like?" Dawn asked. "Was he beautiful?"

I stretched out the details, making the story last. Just the telling of it warmed me, and I could feel Dawn relax in my arms.

When morning light brightened our snow-covered windows, we heard the roar of a snowplow. Then someone rapped on the glass. The Good Samaritan driver took us to my mother's house. "You were out all night in that awful storm?" Mom said. "God must have been watching over you."

I told her about the black dog that saved my life, and she looked doubtful. "I know my road," she said. "There's no such dog around here."

Then her eyes widened. "But, you know, twice I've seen a black wolf wandering around that very spot—" She stopped. She knew it as well as I did. That dog, or wolf, or whatever it was, wasn't wandering. It had been sent.

Midnight Visit

Fred Wickert

DURING MY AIR FORCE CAREER, I was stationed in Tokyo, Japan. While there, I acquired a wife, a dog, and a cat. The dog, a honey-colored cocker spaniel with a lot of white spots on his nose, was named Freckles. We named the cat Blondie; he was yellow and white and had no tail. Fortunately, Freckles and Blondie got along with each other very well.

Freckles and I had a relationship of deep and abiding love. When the Air Force sent my wife and me back to the United States, we were not allowed to bring animals on the plane. I had to send Freckles and Blondie on a commercial flight.

I took the two animals to the airport and put them together in the same cage. They were such good friends that I knew they would be happier and less afraid on the flight if they had each other. People at the airport were amazed when they saw Freckles and Blondie snuggled in the cage side by side. Everybody knows that dogs and cats just don't mix. But these two were the best of friends.

After we picked up Freckles and Blondie upon their safe arrival at the airport in California, they traveled with my wife and me in our car all over the United States. These two animals were always with us.

Halfway through my military career, I was transferred to Andrews Air Force Base, in Maryland, to join the security forces protecting the aircraft used by the president. Freckles and Blondie went with us to this new assignment.

After five years, I went to the war in Vietnam. This time, I had to go alone and leave Freckles and my wife behind. Blondie had passed away two years earlier. When I returned home from Vietnam a little over a year later, Freckles and I were overjoyed to be together again. I had been reassigned to presidential security for the remainder of my career, so we wouldn't have to move again.

In late autumn of the following year, I got up one morning at a very early hour. Freckles woke up and joined me in the kitchen as I prepared and ate my breakfast. I petted him for a few minutes, and then he went to the coat closet inside the front door. The closet contained a folded piece of carpet on which he liked to sleep.

When I was ready to leave for work, I went to get my coat and hat from the closet. I reached down to pet Freckles and tell him good-bye. That is when I discovered that he had died there in the closet. I canceled my plans for the day, built him a nice casket, and gave him a decent burial.

I felt devastated by Freckles' sudden death. He had been my little buddy for so many years, and we had been through much together. I was stunned and shocked by this unanticipated loss, and I grieved for him. My wife and I had no clue that Freckles' time was nearing an end. He was old but had not been ill at all. A happy dog, he had carried out his normal routine and showed no signs of discomfort.

About a year later, I was working the midnight shift in a warm hangar, guarding the president's small airplane. There were three separate aircraft with the presidential seal on their sides parked in the same hangar. One was a Boeing 707. It was the airplane the press and public were most familiar with and usually was referred to as Air Force One. The term Air Force One is the code word and call sign for whichever Air Force aircraft the president is flying on. It is only Air Force One while the president is actually aboard the airplane. The smallest one in the hangar was one that most people were unaware of, a four-engine Lockheed Jet

Star. This is the plane I was guarding that night. The other two planes designated for the president were a C-118 Constellation and a four-engine propeller-driven aircraft used for smaller airports where the runway wouldn't be long enough for a jet aircraft to land. One other Boeing 707 did not have the seal permanently displayed on it and was used only as a backup. Whenever the president went somewhere on the Boeing 707, the backup Boeing 707 was not far away. If for some reason there was a breakdown, they would quickly switch to the backup plane, so the president could stay on schedule. The White House fleet at the time numbered about forty aircraft.

When I worked the midnight shift that night, guarding the Lockheed Jet Star, I sat at a small table near the front of the plane. Everyone who came into this area had to sign in and out. At that hour, I was the only one there. Because of the quiet of the huge, empty aircraft hangar and the late hour, I became drowsy and, quite unintentionally, fell asleep. In the military, falling asleep on guard duty is a severely punishable offense. If you are found sleeping, you are court-martialed or severely punished. This kind of indiscretion would ruin a career and even threaten receiving a pension, no matter how long or illustrious a career you had had. Only three years remained before I would retire and be eligible to collect my pension.

Suddenly, Freckles was there on the table, licking my face. His tongue and presence woke me up. I know it wasn't a dream, because my face was wet with his saliva. I could feel him. It was real. He was there.

Just as I awoke, the security superintendent walked through the door on the other side of the hangar. He occasionally came in the middle of the night to check on the duty guard. Freckles had just saved me and my career.

Yes, Freckles had passed away more than a year before. Yet he was still with me and remained my faithful friend. Now I know that there is life after death. And I know that Freckles is my guardian angel.

Little Buddy

Debbie McNally

EVERY DOG SHOULD HAVE A *loving home. So when my co-worker said she had a golden retriever puppy that needed placement, I racked my brain trying to think of a suitable owner. The very next day my friend Karen mentioned she was looking for a golden retriever for her four-year-old son, Michael, before they moved to Redstone, Colorado. "What luck!" Karen said. "We'll take him!" Angels certainly were looking out for Gilligan! As it turned out, the angels were just getting started. Months later Karen told me this story:*

From the moment Gilligan and Michael met, they were inseparable. They played in the yard together for hours, and explored the "summer path" that led up the mountainside near their house in Redstone. When Michael started kindergarten Gilligan rode to the bus stop with him in his mom's van. And that's where he stayed all day long. Karen tried to tempt him out with toys and treats, but nothing would incite him to budge. Michael's "little buddy" refused to go home without him.

Winters come early in Colorado. By Thanksgiving Karen was periodically running the heat in the van for Gilligan while he waited for the school day to end. It was worth it when Michael climbed in for the ride home. "We played Polar Express at recess!" Michael announced one Friday afternoon in December. "We went to the North Pole!"

Michael hadn't stopped talking about the Santa movie since he saw it with some of his classmates. *It's practically like the North Pole around here*, Karen thought as she turned the van down their snowy street. Redstone had recently gotten another three feet of snow on top of the three feet it already had.

The snow kept Michael from his friends that Saturday. His dad was out of town. Still he had his little buddy. After lunch Michael zipped on his snowsuit, and he and Gilligan went out in the yard. Karen watched them through the kitchen window as she did the dishes. Michael's red snowsuit was bright against the snow. "Keep your gloves on!" she called out when Michael pulled one off. "It's freezing!"

"Okay, Mom!" Michael yelled and slipped it back on. Gilligan bounded around him, burying his nose in the snow. Karen finished up the dishes, then brought a laundry basket from upstairs. Another glance out the window showed Michael tossing Gilligan a snowball by the swing set. Karen loaded the washing machine and started it up.

When she returned to the kitchen window, she didn't see Michael anywhere. Not in the backyard. Not on the swing set. She opened the window. "Michael?" she called.

No answer. Karen went out the side door onto the porch. "Michael?" Again, no answer. Karen stepped into her boots and climbed down into the snowy yard. "Michael! Gilligan! Here, boy!" *Little boys have selective hearing*, she thought as she ran around to the front of the house. No sign of them. *Michael might not come when he's called*, she thought, *but Gilligan always does!*

Karen raced out to the dirt road. Empty in both directions. She ran to the summer path, calling frantically. Karen was shivering without her coat. It was after 3:00 PM. In another hour it would be dark!

She couldn't waste another minute searching by herself. She ran into the house to call Search and Rescue. Then she sat down to wait, praying for an angel to watch over her son. Where had Michael and Gilligan gone?

To the North Pole, of course.

While Karen was loading the washing machine, Michael had gazed up at the mountains around them and gotten an idea. "Let's go see Santa!" he told Gilligan. "He's on top of the mountain, just like in the movie!" Michael didn't have a magical express train to carry him to Santa's workshop, but he was sure he could make it on foot.

The summer path was now covered with deep, crunchy snow. Lifting a booted foot high and plunging it down into the powder, Michael started up the mountain. Gilligan leapt alongside him. If Michael was going on an adventure, Gilligan was going to be right beside him.

Michael was sure they would find Santa on the nearest peak, but as they reached the top, panting, all they saw were a lot of pine trees heavy with snow. "Where's Santa?" Michael cried, crushed with disappointment. Gilligan barked.

Michael was tired and the sky was getting dim, but they had come a long way already. What if Santa was just on the next peak? "When we get to the workshop he can give us a ride back home," Michael assured Gilligan. They trudged on. It got harder and harder for Michael to lift his boots out of the snow.

"Maybe we should see Santa another day," he told Gilligan. He turned around to head back, Gilligan at his heels. Going down the mountain was sure easier than going up. "We'll be home soon," Michael said. "I'm cold." But when the boy and his dog finally reached the bottom, they weren't in the backyard at all. They were on the side of a big road—a highway—with no cars in sight. Snow was piled so high along the sides Michael could barely see over it.

"We need to get to the other side, boy!" he said, his teeth chattering. Michael scrambled over the snow bank and ran across the empty highway, Gilligan at his heels. They clambered over the snow bank on this side. Michael looked around. "We're lost!" he wailed. The boy put his head down and cried. Gilligan settled his warm body beside him and licked the tears from his face.

Burt the truck driver wasn't lost at all. He knew exactly where he was: driving on Route 44, just past Redstone. He brought his flatbed truck smoothly around a bend. He was behind schedule delivering a shipment of snowmobiles stacked neatly in back. Just ahead, he saw something in the road, probably a deer. "Poor thing," Burt muttered. He shifted his foot from the accelerator to the brake and turned the wheel to go around it. But as he got closer he gasped. "That's no deer!"

Burt brought his truck to a stop beside the animal. A golden retriever lying right in the road. Burt put on his flashers. The dog must have been hit by a car. Maybe it wasn't too late to save its life. "Don't worry, boy," Burt said as he hopped off the truck. "We'll get you some help."

Before Burt could reach him, the golden retriever jumped off the ground. He wasn't hurt at all. In fact, he had more energy than any dog Burt had ever seen. While Burt tried to get a hold of him, the dog jumped up and down around him. "Hold on, doggie!" Burt said. "You might be hurt. Let me take a look at you!"

The dog was having none of it. When Burt tried to get near, the strange dog ran to the side of the road and barked for all he was worth. "I feel like I'm in a Lassie movie," Burt muttered. The dog honestly seemed to want him to follow. So Burt followed the dog to the edge of the road and peered over the snow bank. A little boy in a red snowsuit was curled up in a ball, shivering.

Karen was just leaving the house to join the Search and Rescue team when the phone rang.

"Mrs. Kashnig?" a man asked.

"Yes. Who is this?"

"My name's Burt," the man said. "I just found a young boy and his friend on Route 44. The boy's name is Michael and his buddy is Gilligan."

Karen's knees nearly buckled in relief. And she didn't feel much steadier as Burt explained just how he'd found Michael on that snowy night. If it hadn't been for Gilligan lying in wait in the road, Burt never would have stopped his truck.

That night, Karen sat Michael down for a serious talk about leaving the backyard. His adventure had taught Michael a lesson. It taught his mother and me something too: Luck hadn't brought Gilligan to Michael's family; angels had. Angels who knew that one day Michael would need Gilligan just as much as Gilligan needed him.

To Sir, With Love

Joan Wester Anderson

BILL AND MARCIA HOLTON AND their children lived on a wheat farm in Oregon; Marcia's parents, Verne and Kay, lived next door. The two family homes were at the bottom of Juniper Canyon, with some of the wheat fields on top of the hill behind the houses. "Our neighbors out here are spread apart, and the nearest town is Helix, ten miles from our ranch," Marcia said. Sometimes it seemed as if they were the only people on earth.

Occasionally Marcia got a little lonely, but she was a woman of faith who prayed regularly that God would watch over her family. So far God had not disappointed her. It was a beautiful Sunday afternoon in early spring, and Marcia had flung open the kitchen door, put boots on the kids so they could run wherever they wanted, and gone outside with them. The sun and promise of warmth were all around them, and planting had begun. Marcia loved this time of year.

"Mommy, look!" Her six-year-old was pointing to the top of the hill behind the house. Marcia gasped. There was an animal the size of a minivan up there, sitting calmly and looking down at them. It was huge, at least two hundred pounds. A bear? Marcia thought not—its fur was yellow and fluffy. A mountain lion? "Walk real slowly toward the house," she whispered to the children. "Wait there, and don't come back until I tell you." Then Marcia took a careful step toward the animal. She knew she would have to investigate it before she'd feel safe letting the children play outside again.

As she got closer, Marcia could hardly believe her eyes. It was a dog! The biggest dog she had ever seen, probably part mastiff, part Saint Bernard. Where had he come from? She knew all the dogs in the Helix area, and no one owned one like this. Was he friendly? "Here, boy..." she put out a tentative hand.

As if he had been given permission, the dog got up and trotted down the hill, directly to Marcia, tail sweeping the driveway. He allowed himself to be petted, his ears to be scratched and—once she had called the children over to him—hugged and ridden on.

"Isn't he nice?" Marcia said. "What shall we name him?"

"I think we should call him 'Sir'," one of the children suggested. "Because he deserves respect."

He did seem regal. Now all that was needed was Bill's permission to keep him. The family could hardly wait until he got home from plowing.

"Oh, come on—he won't eat much," Marcia teased that night. "Look at him—isn't he cute?

"'Cute' isn't a word I'd use," Bill responded. Sir reminded him more of lions he had seen in zoos.

"But he seems to know us, Daddy," the five-year-old pointed out. "As if he's always lived here." Everyone stared at Sir, who seemed to be following the conversation, his massive head moving from one person to another.

"Well..." Bill was weakening. Although his in-laws had two blue-heeler dogs to help with the cattle they raised, Bill's family had never owned one. Yet what better place for such a big dog than a ranch? "But we'd have to advertise in the 'Lost and Found' in case he belongs to anyone," Bill said. "And if we have to give him back, I don't want you all to be sad." Everyone cheered and agreed.

*   *   *

THIS CABBIE PROBABLY DIDN'T KNOW *it was his final Sunday on earth*, Paul Smith (not his real name) mused, as he lounged in the backseat, his pistol pointed at the hijacked driver's head. But he wasn't going to leave any witnesses to this last robbery. The clerk in the Walla Walla convenience store hadn't seen his face—he'd locked her in the storage closet before he emptied the cash register. But it wasn't much cash, and he was going to have to pull another job soon.

Most important, however, was finding a spot where he could hide for a while. He was an escaped convict on the run, and out here in Oregon the little homesteads were so few and far between that he could easily dispose of the residents, then portray himself as a visiting relative or friend if any nosy neighbor happened by. Eventually he'd commandeer another car and driver, just like this one, and set out again, working his way east. The police would never find him if he stayed out of sight for a while.

The cab driver's hands were shaking. "I-I know you told me not to talk," he said, "but we've gone sixty miles, and my gas gauge is on E. I was already low when you pulled the gun on me..."

Paul Smith looked out the window. They were passing a wheat field, which looked down into a canyon. At the bottom were two houses. He could see no other dwelling around for miles in any direction. Perfect. He could wait up here until dark. "Turn into this field," he told the driver, who obeyed just as the engine began to sputter. If anyone in those houses did hear the shot, Smith reflected, they would probably assume it was just a hunter bringing down a rabbit. He looked at the terrified cabbie and reached for his gun.

It was a perfect set-up; later, from his perch on top of the hill, he watched the families move about the two houses. At times, it looked as if the two women and the little kids were alone. He considered strategies. He could go down now, surprise and overpower the women and children, or he could wait until dark when the men would probably be back, break into one of the houses and take command of everyone at the same time. But he couldn't afford to make a mistake in judgment, because he had very few bullets left. Ultimately, he had to get far away from here, before the authorities in Washington figured out where he had gone.

It would have to be tonight, when they were asleep and unprepared.

* * *

MEANWHILE, THE HOLTONS WERE DEBATING whether Sir should sleep in the house or the barn. But the massive canine settled down easily on the porch across the back door threshold, as if he'd always done so. There was no point in trying to move him, and quiet eventually descended on the household. Until a little after midnight. Then Sir started to bark. At first it was just a few short yaps, followed by growling, then howling.

"Sir, stop it!" Bill called through the open screened window.

Sir obeyed, but a few minutes later the whole process started again.

"What is the matter with that dog?" Bill asked irritably. He got up again and looked out the windows of the porch door. There was no sign of a wild animal. It wasn't that unusual for a coyote or badger to run through the yard and set off a brief chorus of barking from the dogs next door. But tonight their in-laws' dogs were absolutely quiet.

"Maybe he's homesick?" Marcia suggested.

"Wouldn't he be whining?" Bill asked. "This sounds more like aggressiveness. Sir, be quiet."

Again, Sir obeyed, but only for a moment. He refused to leave the back door, wanting to go in search of what was bothering him. But he also barked and growled continuously, as if he were keeping something at bay. It was almost dawn before the adults in the two households all fell asleep. "None of us were very happy with Sir or me that morning," Marcia recalled. "But we all agreed to try him one more night."

That day Marcia and the children played with Sir continuously. Wherever they went on the ranch—into the barn, across the road—he accompanied them. "When we were in the house, Sir would lie in front of the door. Nothing could get him to move, until we came out of the house again."

That night, Sir barked only a few times. Marcia relaxed. He was settling into his new home, and she was delighted about it. She loved him and depended on him already in a way she had never thought she could.

*   *   *

A FEW DAYS LATER MARCIA'S dad, Verne, was on his way to town when he passed one of the wheat fields and saw something shining, looking like a car windshield. There shouldn't be any cars there. Verne drove closer until he spotted a taxi with Washington state license plates on it. Something was definitely wrong, but he wasn't about to investigate by himself. He turned around, drove home, and called the state police. "Get your family, your rifle, and lock yourself in one of the houses. And don't open the door for anyone," he was told. The police were on their way.

Slowly over the next several hours as the authorities investigated, Marcia, Bill, and their folks absorbed the shocking story. On Sunday an escaped convict who had just robbed a convenience store had forced a cab driver to take him just past Helix, where he then murdered the cab driver.

The sheriff took Marcia and Bill up the hill, about one hundred feet from their back porch, and pointed to footprints, several cigarette butts, and a discarded cigarette package. Marcia was shocked. The killer had obviously stood here in the dark; waiting for a chance to come down and . . . she didn't want to think about it.

But why hadn't he done so? "I think the only thing that saved all of you was that dog sticking to you like glue," the sheriff said. "If Smith was running low on bullets and had to get past Sir's attack before he could get to you . . ."

"He'd also lose the element of surprise," Bill commented. He had complained about Sir's noisiness. But what would have happened to all of them if Sir had not warned the criminal away? What would have happened if they had not adopted Sir?

No one knew where Paul Smith had gone. Later, it was discovered that he had flagged down another farmer, taken him hostage, and repeated the scenario across the country. He killed one more person before he was caught in Pittsburgh about a week after he had left the Holton farm. Immediately, he was sent back to prison in Washington. Sir stayed with the Holtons for about a year before everyone sensed it was time for him to move on. Ultimately, he went to live at the fire station in town.

Why was the Holton family spared and not the unfortunate hostages? Another mystery, for we know that God loved them all. But "in the Bible, it tells us that if we pray, God provides angels for our protection," Marcia said. Perhaps Sir was not really an angel. But Marcia has no doubts that he was sent by angels.

The Dolphins Saved My Life

Anne Archer Butcher

IT WAS CHRISTMAS VACATION, AND I went home for the holiday to visit my mother on Hilton Head Island, South Carolina. I loved coming to the island. It renewed my sense of self and restored my health. Here I felt connected to my roots, nature, and the vast oceans. At the time of this visit, on Christmas Day, I had graduated from college and was teaching high school. I loved my work, but it was very demanding physically, emotionally, and mentally. The island was a sanctuary where I felt that the universe might actually hear my call for renewal. I longed to just dive into the ocean and swim until I could swim no more. I wanted to vent my energies and relax totally. I was always a strong swimmer, and my family had called me a fish because I taught myself how to swim at age two. As a child, I'd swim long distances, staying in the water all day and loving every minute of it.

Around noon on this holiday, I went to the beach and walked alone on the warm sands along the water's edge. The sun was brilliant, but most people sitting on the beach probably thought the water was too cool for swimming. Vacationers on this international island resort greeted me with a variety of accents as I gathered shells.

When I felt warm enough, I walked into the ocean waves and dove in. I swam hard and fast. Even when I felt tired, I continued. At last I rolled over on my back and looked toward the beach. I was amazed to be so far from the shore. The people on the beach were tiny specks, and a large expanse of ocean waves separated us.

This had been my family home for years, so I knew these waters well. My mind raced to warnings I'd received. The few sharks that had ever been sighted in this area were known to be attracted to shrimp boats, but none was in sight. Even though no one else was in the water, I didn't feel frightened.

I began my long swim back with strong strokes. I loved the smell of the fresh salt air. The water's temperature had become comfortable. I swam with total abandon until I again checked the shoreline. It was as if I had barely moved. I could feel myself being pulled out to sea. Trying not to panic, I reminded myself that people watching me from the shore had probably seen how far I'd gone out.

Suddenly, I was frozen with fear because off to my left a dark fin moved directly toward me. My heart pounded wildly. I stopped swimming and attempted to float and bob in the water, stretching out like a log on the surface. I could barely breathe. I closed my eyes. I tried desperately to keep my mind from entertaining the horrors of being eaten by a shark. Suddenly, a powerful, smooth, sleek body rose underneath me.

I couldn't imagine what was happening. I felt my body being lifted slightly. While gliding across the water's surface, I was being moved toward the shore. Then slowly, gently, I was lowered back into the ocean. But immediately, I felt again the strange sensation of a powerful body rising up, then lifting and carrying me forward.

The surface of the water broke in front of me and I could finally see the creature who had been carrying me. It was a beautiful dolphin who jumped through the air, looked at me, dived to the left, and dipped under the water again. All the while, I was moved through the water at great speed as another of these wonderful animals carried me on his back. Soon, a school of dolphins was circling all around me. One at a time they moved beneath me, each lifting and gradually carrying me back toward shore as if they were performing an orchestrated dance or choreographed ballet.

After each dolphin took his turn carrying me, he then leaped in front and swam around to begin again. One to the left. One to the right. Quickly and smoothly, they brought me to chest-high water. Then they encircled me, spinning, diving, smiling. The dolphins called out in an amazing, high-pitched language that filled me with delight. I clapped in appreciation for the show they were providing. Touched and in awe, I couldn't stop talking to and thanking them. Eventually, they turned, said farewell, and danced out to sea.

By this time, a crowd of people had gathered on the shore. They'd seen the dark fin and anticipated a shark attack. After watching my incredible return on the backs of frolicking dolphins, they greeted me, laughing, talking, and asking about how the dolphins had rescued me. What a memorable moment. We were a group of people from all over the world who had somehow come together to witness something none of us would ever forget. It was a marvelous gift on this special Christmas Day.

The dolphins helped me relate to the blessings of nature as I had never before. I became more aware that all life is connected by a divine thread of love. Totally renewed in spirit, I felt confident that the universe supports me.

Just Another Stray?

Barbara Wernecke Durkin

WHEN I WAS GROWING UP in a small town-house apartment in suburban Baltimore in the 1950s there never seemed to be enough room in our household. Yet Mom always found just a little more. That's because she and Dad took in strays—stray people, that is, for the most part.

It was bad enough, I felt, all of us living on top of one another when the boarders were our relations—distant cousins that Mom was always welcoming. We weren't rich or even well off. Somehow, though, Mom made the meals stretch so that everyone not only got to eat but enjoyed seconds. It always reminded me of the parable of loaves and fishes.

"Why do you do it?" I'd ask her as we washed the dinner dishes, a titanic labor I resented only slightly less than constantly having to surrender my room to visitors. "Don't they have anywhere else to go? Can't they at least eat before they barge in on us?"

Mom would smile, her face tired but cheerful. "Well, my mother used to take people in, especially when times were hard, and your father loves everyone. Besides, you never know."

"Never know what, Mom?"

"They might be angels."

"Angels?" I cried. "Angels?" Then I started giggling, thinking of the motley parade through our home. Mom laughed too.

"Well," she repeated, playfully flicking soap bubbles at me, "you never know."

I grew up, and inevitably began finding my own strays—or at least they found me. Several of my college friends who had financial hardships came to live with us, even after Dad died and Mom and I were struggling to make ends meet. Oddly, the less we had, the more Mom wanted to share.

I finished college, got married and had kids—and a house—of my own. As Mom got old, her mind began to fail and she slipped in and out of reality. How heartbreaking to see this woman who could bear so many burdens slowly growing confused and helpless! She lived with us, since I couldn't stand for her to go to a nursing home until it was absolutely necessary.

She had good days when she was practically her old self, but on others she stared out the window and asked in a trembling voice, "Where are we now?" Sometimes she roamed in search of mythical clumps of giant raspberries to make the jams and cakes she used to feed visitors. I would have to go looking for her as dusk fell, calling her name in the woods that abutted our parcel of land.

Late one night I fell apart. "I can't watch her twenty-four hours a day," I said to my husband, fighting off tears of frustration and self-pity. "I don't know what to do."

Bill held me and murmured words of comfort in my ear. I always felt so soothed wrapped in his arms. But that night I couldn't stop crying. After Bill went to sleep I got down on my knees and prayed before collapsing into bed exhausted.

My mind was still a bit agitated the next evening when I pulled into our driveway and saw an animal—a rather large dog—trotting unhurriedly from our backyard into the sweep of my headlights.

"Hey!" I shouted out the window. "Scat!" I didn't want some stray mutt scaring Mom or bothering the cats. "Get lost!"

The dog looked at me unflinchingly. How galling! He was supposed to be afraid of me. Instead he seemed pleased to stand his ground in my headlights, like an actor at center stage, staring me down. I'd heard tales of wild dogs rampaging through the woods. "Bill!" I shouted and leaned on the horn until he came out. My husband had a way with dogs. "We have a visitor," I told him as he came outside, shrugging on an old jean jacket.

"Hi, buddy," Bill called in a calm, friendly voice, walking slowly toward the animal with his hand held low. "How ya' doin', big guy?" Ears back, the dog allowed Bill to approach. He sniffed Bill's hand and smiled.

That's not a figure of speech. The dog grinned at my husband.

"He's glad to be here," Bill explained as the dog wagged his tail and curled around my husband's leg.

"Oh?" I was skeptical. "Let's see how happy he is to see the cats."

Bill examined the dog's coat and paws, and said, "He's pretty worn out. His pads look kind of ragged, like he's come a long way. I bet he's starving."

"All dogs are starving."

"C'mon, boy. Let's go inside and get something to eat."

I followed them in, complaining all the way. "Just what I need," I moaned. The cats scattered. "Another character to feed and clean up after. All we've got is cat food."

"It'll do," Bill said, scrounging under the sink for an old bowl. "I'm sure he's not picky."

He sure wasn't. He wolfed down the whole can. I gave him seconds.

"I think he needs to stay the night," said Bill as we watched the animal lick the edges of the bowl.

"That mangy fleabag is not staying in this house."

"Just for the night," Bill went on, oblivious to my concern. He disappeared down the basement steps and came up with an old blanket that he fluffed and laid out by the fireplace in the family room. The dog seemed to know it was for him. He circled in the center, plopped down, and with a sigh was fast asleep.

The next morning Bill stopped in the kitchen to grab his coffee and make a plea for our overnight visitor. I had just gotten the kids off to school. They wanted to hang on to the stray too. "We should think about keeping him, Barbara. I saw your mom talking to him this morning. Why don't you run him by the vet to see if he's got any health problems we should know about?"

I shook my head. "I can't deal with another problem. I've reached my limit."

Bill gave the dog a scratch. "Look at what intelligent eyes he has." I tried not to look. "Maybe you'll like him more after you spend a day with him. See ya."

Bill flew out the door. The dog was grinning at me again. He certainly seemed intelligent, as if he knew he had to work on my resolve. He had a kind of nobility that you see in some dogs, as if he might be a king in disguise. I scraped some egg and bacon and other tasty scraps into his bowl along with the cat food. "I'm sorry I called you mangy," I said. "You're not so bad."

Later, out in the yard, I kneeled down and took a good look at him in the bright morning sunlight. He was exceptionally long-legged, part retriever, part shepherd, and part something I couldn't identify. His coat shone like spun gold. His face was handsome. I looked into his glistening eyes. He seemed to be looking right into me. We remained that way for a while, just staring. Then I asked, "You want to stay with us?"

Immediately he backed away and kind of tossed his head from side to side. I'd never seen a dog do that. "You don't want to be our new dog?" I asked. He did a little jump, then nuzzled my hand and thumped his tail against my leg. He was trying to tell me something.

"What is it?"

He turned away from me, and to my complete amazement trotted quite purposefully and precisely around the perimeter of our property. At each corner he paused, looked directly at me and actually nodded his head—a deliberate movement he repeated each time. I was, to say the least, agog. After completing his tour he returned and sat at my side, stock-still. At that moment I heard it. As clearly and truly as a bell, I heard these unmistakable words: This property is blessed; this property is safe. No harm shall come here.

I gasped, looking around for the source. Had it been a trick of the wind? No, the words had been too clear. The dog, of course, had not spoken. My hand rested on the back of his neck, feeling the warmth of his thick, deep coat between my fingers. I was overcome with a sense of love and peace, an unfathomable experience of relief, as if the world had been lifted from my shoulders and I could breathe again. At once I understood: The words were a promise from God, delivered by one of His trusted messengers.

The dog rose to his feet. With a last look he loped off, his long legs carrying him with impressive agility. He turned around once, his tail like a flag in the spring breeze. Then he was gone, mission accomplished.

Since that day I've led my life with a tremendous sense of assurance that no matter what happens, God will be there. Our home has weathered storms and a rash of neighborhood burglaries untouched. My mother lived with us safely until her time came. When I think about that strange and wondrous creature who visited us, I always remember that Mom thought an angel might be among the strays she collected.

"You never know," she liked to say.

You never do.

Amber's Angels

Elizabeth Purdy

THE ROUGH MILE-LONG PATH to the front door of our new home meandered over the hills, creeks, and cattle guards of a neglected country estate. Vegetation threatened to engulf the abandoned mansion along the way. The run-down condition of the 1,400-acre spread had been a big reason we'd been able to rent the estate manager's old house for a pittance. I loved the peaceful isolation of the countryside. Our three little ones—a newborn, an eighteen-month-old and a three-year-old—were too young to be affected by our move, but I worried that it might be a difficult transition for Amber, who would start at a new school in the fall.

Even with bargain rent we struggled to get by. My husband took construction and drywall jobs wherever he could get them, working sixty-hour weeks, often during nights and weekends. The children required at least the same amount of time from me, and I appreciated Amber's eagerness to help. She loved to be a little mommy. Her independent spirit made it easy to let her look after herself. Still, I worried. She was, after all, only six. Someone had to look out for her too.

When it was time to sign up Amber for kindergarten, she was excited. I couldn't help thinking, though, that with her spending all day in a classroom I would be there for her even less.

On the first day of school, Amber trotted downstairs in her new plaid skirt, white blouse and kneesocks. Her wispy brown hair curled around her face, setting off her big, dark eyes. She had gotten ready all by herself and waited patiently while I settled the three little ones into the car.

In the mornings, I could drive her down the rugged trail to our mailbox and wait for the school bus with her. But in the afternoons the babies would be napping, and I couldn't leave them. Amber understood that when the school bus dropped her off she would have to make the mile-long walk home alone.

"Hon, I'll be waiting on the front porch when you get here," I assured her with a kiss as the bus approached. She hopped on, waved, and was gone.

Throughout the day I pictured Amber sitting at a small desk, coloring, reciting the alphabet, and playing with new friends. She'll be fine, I told myself. But as I stepped out onto the porch that afternoon, I realized with a start that the red speck streaking across the far hilltop must be Amber. Her little legs pumping, she tore through the overgrown weeds along the path. As she got closer, I could hear her hysterical cries. Her eyes were wide with terror.

"Sweetie, I'm right here," I said, darting across the yard.

"*Mawwwwmy!*" she wailed, flinging herself into my arms. "I can't walk home all by myself!" she choked. "I can't!"

I hugged her until she caught her breath, then smoothed her hair. Her face was streaked with tears, and one sock sagged around her ankle.

That night when I read from the Bible to the children, I made a point to choose verses about courage and protection. Then I said good night to the babies and sat on the edge of Amber's bed.

"I know it can be scary to walk home all by yourself," I said, tucking the blankets around her. "But God is looking out for you, and so am I." She nodded, and I kissed her forehead and smoothed her hair before turning out the light.

The next morning as we drove down to the bus stop, I told her, "Remember, I'll be waiting on the porch for you."

I hoped Amber's journey would be less frightening for her, having done it once already. Around three o'clock I pushed open the screen door.

Minutes later Amber tumbled into the yard, in tears again. Each day thereafter was no better. I felt guilty standing on the porch, straining my eyes to see her sprinting over the hill half a mile from home. There had to be a way to make this easier.

My husband and I decided to take a family trip down the lane that weekend. We dressed the kids in jackets and boots and spent most of an afternoon going up the drive to the mailbox, where the bus dropped off Amber, and back down again to the front yard. Along the way we picked up leaves drenched in the hues of autumn and pointed out that the most beautiful ones had fallen from the tallest trees. We tottered over the bars of the cattle guards, showing Amber how to keep her balance and walk sideways across them so her toes wouldn't slip through. We named the cows and sang songs. We even caught a butterfly. I held it carefully in the palm of my hand as Amber looked in amazement. We toured the dilapidated old mansion, investigated the woods, splashed across streams and scrambled up the biggest hill. I'd never realized how rugged the path could be on foot! All day Amber toughed it out with us, most of the time as our fearless little leader. If only her security would last when we couldn't be with her.

Amber made it to the porch without sobbing on Monday, but within a couple days her fears of snakes in the water and creatures in the woods had returned. "There are ghosts in the mansion," she complained. "And the trees are big and mean." What else could I do?

Then one night I was reading out loud from the Old Testament when Amber asked what angels were. I hadn't really thought about angels in a while and took a moment before answering. "God uses angels to protect us from harm. He calls upon them to watch over us."

Her eyes bright, she exclaimed, "Let's pray for angels to be with me when I walk home from school!" So we did. Amber prayed for her angels, and I prayed that God would not let her down.

The next afternoon I put the little ones in bed for their naps and went out to the porch. *Lord, we're counting on You*, I prayed. *Please, send angels for Amber.* I waited, a knot in my stomach.

As soon as I saw her crest the hill, I noticed something odd. Amber was not running. She wasn't even in a hurry. What had gotten into her? From my vantage point she seemed to be skipping or even dancing across the grassy hilltops. And something was moving along with her.

Butterflies! Hundreds, perhaps thousands, arced above her in a satiny canopy. Amber stopped to twirl under them before they floated to the ground like a carpet laid out before her. She seemed to be laughing as she tiptoed to the edge. Instantly the butterflies rose up and over her as one wide swath and took a gentle lead. They fluttered farther up the hill then glided down again. Amber scampered up to meet them, and they hovered over her as before, then drifted ahead.

Repeating this pattern up and down the hillside, then through the woods, and over streams, the delicate flight escorted Amber right to her own front yard, where as one they rose for the last time and flew high over the mountain behind our house and scattered.

"Did you see them, Mommy?" Amber asked, jumping up and down. "Did you see my angels? When I got off the bus they were by the mailbox, waiting for me." I hugged Amber to me. "I'm never going to be afraid to walk home again." She bounded up the porch steps. I wanted to tell Amber that I wasn't going to be afraid either. The angels were there for me too. A good mother does the best she can, I think, and a smart one knows that God sends angels—wings aflutter—to look after the rest.

Angel's Miracle

Jan Nash

I ADOPTED A TWO-YEAR-OLD poodle/terrier mix from our local shelter, and named her Angel. She came from another shelter as a stray who had been abused. Angel was very skinny, extremely shy, and afraid of everyone. I fell in love with her immediately. Since I have multiple sclerosis, I believed that this dog would be perfect for me. We would take care of each other.

I live alone in a high-rise building on Lake Superior with other seniors and disabled tenants. Within weeks, with lots of love, patience, and socializing with neighbors and pets, Angel became a totally different dog.

My little soul mate is now the happiest and most popular dog in the building. She loves everybody, giving kisses to everyone she sees. She never misbehaves, snaps, or barks at anyone. Angel brings her favorite toy or treat to me when I'm feeling bad, or she jumps on my bed and whines until I lie down. She then lies beside me.

One night, Angel became restless and woke me up. I rarely go out late at night, as Angel uses a puppy pad after dark. This time, though, because of her odd behavior, I decided to get dressed and take her out. She was whining and seemed anxious.

I took her around to the parking lot side of our building, back by our garage. She always stays by me, either on or off the leash, but this time she pulled as hard as she could and whined. I unhooked her leash, thinking she must have to go badly. Instead of running to the grass, Angel hurried into the parking lot and darted between two vehicles. I found her sitting next to Wayne, one of our tenants, who was on the ground. He lay in a fetal position with his walker nearby.

I stooped down to ask what had happened. Not fully conscious, Wayne mumbled that he had fallen. He wore shorts and a light jacket, although it was thirty-eight degrees. He couldn't move. He said he'd recently had surgery on both knees and was in a lot of pain.

I feared he might have also broken something. After calling 911, I asked him how long he had been lying on the cold pavement. He said, "About an hour, I think."

I squeezed my knees under Wayne's head to lift it off the ground. He was freezing, so I tried to cover him with my body and coat. We stayed like this, with Angel near him, until the police and ambulance arrived. The paramedics quickly transferred Wayne to a gurney and bundled him in warm blankets. Soon he was on his way to the hospital.

I have no idea how Angel knew about the injured tenant. We live on the eleventh floor, and our apartment faces the lake. Our windows were closed, and I had a small fan running.

The next day, I called the hospital and talked to Wayne. He told me he had suffered a severe heart attack and had no idea why he was outside by his van at that hour. He kept thanking me. I told him it was God and Angel he should thank.

Au Revoir, Floppy

Richard Williams as told to Rich Saladin

In June of last year the Williams family reunion took place. The high point for me was when one of my aunts gave Grandpa Richard a present. He dug into the box and pulled out a stuffed rabbit. My aunt said, "We wanted it to be a reminder of... well, you know." I wondered what a grown man would want with such a gift. My grandfather stroked the animal's ears, then his eyes took on a faraway look as he recounted a story I'd never heard him tell:

Back in 1944 I was just twenty-two. Unlike a lot of boys my age, I didn't run off to join the service. My father wasn't well and needed help on the farm. When I was drafted, though, I went without a fuss. I didn't know what I was in for until I got to Normandy. The bodies littering the beach horrified me.

By the time the 35th Division pushed on into France and set up position on a hilltop in Mortagne a couple weeks later, I was shaking from fatigue. I'd been trained in field artillery, and my job was to load a hundred-pound shells into the howitzer. Hefting shell after shell into the big gun was backbreaking work. We got no rest for the next eight days and nights, as we tried to hold the hill. We'd been surrounded by the Germans, and it was nonstop bombs, bullets, blood and screams.

I slid into a foxhole and wondered how my squad of twelve men—mostly farm boys like me, scared and exhausted—would make it. *Please, God,* I prayed, *protect us.* I poked my head up to check the enemy's movements and saw something bounce a few feet in front of me. I hit the ground and held my helmet. No explosion. I waited a few minutes and poked my head up again. It was a rabbit! A pure white rabbit with floppy ears. It hopped around the hill, almost as if it were inspecting each battery of men.

"You guys see that?" I yelled.

"Yeah," Biff Barker yelled back. "What's a white rabbit doing here? I thought this place only had those brown hares."

The rabbit entertained us for a while and then hopped away. The rest of that day, whenever there was a break in the fighting, we collapsed in foxholes and talked about the rabbit. That got us trading stories about animals we'd known growing up, then about our lives at home and our beliefs. We were Protestants, Catholics, Jews and even some atheists, but found we had so much in common that for a little while, at least, it seemed we weren't on a battlefield in France anymore.

The next day the Germans retreated, and the captain called, "CSMO!" (Close Station, Move Out.) We'd just loaded the last of our equipment when one of the guys said, "Hey, look! It's that crazy rabbit."

Sure enough, the white rabbit was hopping around nearby. When Biff tossed a shovel into the equipment cage, the bunny hopped right onto his foot and looked up at him. "You want to go with us, little guy?" Biff asked. Then he glanced at Sergeant Ross.

"Go ahead," the sarge grunted. "Put him in the cage."

We took the rabbit to our next position, where I opened up the equipment-cage door. "End of the line," I said. The bunny hopped out, paraded down the line of trucks and across a meadow. As I watched him go off into the countryside, I realized how much the land back home looked like this.

But it didn't look the same after eight more days of shelling. Again, with little or no sleep, we held fast to our high-ground position. Suddenly, one of the guys down the line started waving and pointing. I snatched my binoculars. There was something weaving in the long grass. *What is that?* Not big enough to be a person. And then I saw a flash of white fur. I felt all the tension drain from me. When the fighting stopped, as far down the line as I could see guys were smiling as they pointed at the white rabbit.

Minutes later the captain yelled, "CSMO!" Once again, as we loaded up, the bunny hopped around our feet expectantly until someone put him in the equipment cage. One of the men said, "I wonder where he goes when he's not with us." The rabbit seemed to take pretty good care of himself. When we unloaded later that day he hopped off toward the woods, bouncing so high we could see him from hundreds of yards away. We couldn't help but laugh at the spunky little show-off. At the same time, we hoped he wouldn't get himself killed.

Days later the rabbit reappeared, livelier than ever. A big whoop went up. Again when the captain called CSMO, the rabbit was eager to get back into the equipment cage. "Looks like we've got ourselves a mascot," someone said. "Now he needs a name." With his big ears, it seemed natural to call him Floppy, or Flop for short. We passed the word, and at our next stop guys from all the other trucks called out his name as he hopped down the line. We busted out laughing when one guy yelled, "Let's not say good-bye, let's just say *au revoir*, Floppy!"

The war took on a new viciousness when winter settled in. We fired our guns around the clock, trying to support the troops at the front. Our fingers were raw from working the cold steel howitzers, and I don't know how long we were in the field before a supply truck finally got to us with overcoats, ponchos and gloves.

One night as I stood guard, it poured down rain. I pulled my hood tighter around my head. With the howling wind I was afraid I might not hear the enemy approach. *Help me, God, to protect those in my care right now*, I prayed. Just then I heard a soupy plop…plop…plop. I got my rifle free of my poncho and shouted, "Who goes there?" Something landed on my foot. I snapped on the flashlight and there in the beam I saw Flop.

"Hey, buddy, be careful," I told him. "I might've killed you." He hopped away as if he didn't have a care in the world. I realized that if I'd heard something as small as a rabbit, I'd have no trouble hearing a person. "Thanks, Flop!" I yelled after him.

Flop always had that uncanny sense of timing. Without fail he'd appear and minutes later the captain would call for us to move out. No matter how severe the weather or how grisly the combat, Flop stayed with us. When the war finally started to wind down, we were in Germany. Traveling along the Elbe River one night, the sarge told us to pull over and take a ten-minute break. We jumped out of the half-track, and I went to the equipment cage to check on Flop.

"I can't believe it. He's asleep." I opened the cage and picked him up. Gently I placed him on the ground. "Stretch your legs, Flop," I encouraged him. But he just lay there.

By then guys had started to gather. Biff shone a light on Flop. "He's barely breathing," the sarge said. "I think he's dying."

"Let's make him a nest so he can be comfortable," I said. The squad gathered long grass, twisted it into a thick bunch and put it at the base of a tree. Flop looked so tiny when we placed him in the nest. We pulled the sides up high, hoping that would keep predators from spotting him. One guy poured some water into his mess-kit bowl and left it near the nest. "Just in case," he said quietly.

"Move out!" the sarge bellowed. The mood was somber as we jostled along. "Strange to be traveling without Flop," someone finally said. "He's been with us back since Mortagne, when we were surrounded by Germans."

"Yeah. That was two hundred and seventy days ago," I said, ever mindful of how long I'd been away from home.

At daybreak we set our guns and ammo up in record time, then hightailed it back to where we'd left Flop. The twelve of us quietly approached the nest. Biff was the first one to get close. "He's not here!" he said. We searched the area for Flop, but the sarge ordered us to give up after three hours.

Back in the half-track the questions came: Where'd he go? How could he have moved when he had barely been breathing? The water hadn't been touched, and the nest was intact, and there was no fur or blood, so another animal hadn't gotten to him. What happened?

"Maybe he was our guardian angel," one guy said.

"You know," Biff replied, "I don't think our division has lost a man since Flop came."

"He's right," the sarge agreed. "Had a few wounded, but no one seriously hurt."

We all thought about that quietly until Biff asked if he could lead us in prayer. Together—Protestants, Catholics, Jews and even the atheists—we bowed our heads. "Heavenly Father," Biff prayed, "Flop came out of nowhere and went the same way. Thank You for the pleasure of his company, and for Your continued protection of all of us."

Our reunion was the first and last time I heard Grandpa Richard tell that story. He died recently, and though that makes me sad, I know he's okay. The stuffed rabbit we gave him last June reminds me that God is always with us in some way, our comfort until we get home safe and sound.

Angel in the Cemetery

Joan Wester Anderson

SEVENTY-ONE-YEAR-OLD WILLIAM DOUBLER'S family was shocked when he was diagnosed with colon caner in November and given six months to live. William and his wife were people of great faith. "We set up a hospice for Dad at their home," their daughter, Mary Frank, said, "and each day I would come in and we'd have a prayer vigil. Even though there was great pain at the thought of losing him, there was more pain as we watched his suffering increase." That was why, when William died only six weeks after his diagnosis, Mary felt relief as well as loss.

"None of us was expecting it," she said. "We had planned a last Christmas together and now even that wouldn't happen."

Everyone in their close-knit family grieved, but Mary's younger sister, Marilyn Wakenight, was inconsolable. "I was sick a lot when I was little," Marilyn said, "and Dad was my constant companion. As I grew, I became a tomboy and accompanied Dad while he did chores. I just couldn't imagine life without him."

It was a somber Christmas. The Doubler family had decided to hold the funeral services over until the following week, so that the out-of-town relatives and friends could observe Christmas with their own families. It was a considerable gesture, but it also had the effect of keeping everyone in a state of intense mourning. Marilyn wept constantly, and Mary began to worry about her. Marilyn hadn't been able to attend the family prayer vigils to prepare as the others had. She needed a sign that Dad had not left them forever. In fact, they all needed a sign.

William's wake was on a Friday afternoon and evening, and Marilyn went back to the funeral home after everyone had left, to spend some quiet time with her father. The funeral was on Saturday, and afterward the Doublers hosted a luncheon for all the family and guests. Again, Marilyn slipped away. *Where is she going now?* Mary wondered, concerned. She was just about to send out some people to look for Marilyn when she reappeared at the luncheon. Mary was surprised. Her sister looked almost happy.

"You've got to see this!" Marilyn announced to the remaining group. "There is a dog lying on top of Dad's grave! When he saw me, he jumped up and kept on licking my face. I want to take him something to eat—he looks like he's hungry." She gathered a plate of meat and other tidbits. Mary looked at her mother, and both women reached for their coats. If a stray dog would make Marilyn feel better, they'd encourage her.

In the freezing afternoon, eight people drove to the cemetery. "And as Marilyn had described, there was a dog laying on top of Dad's grave," Mary said. "He looked like a large mixed-breed collie, red, brown, and white, and he didn't have a collar or tags. When Marilyn got out of the car and climbed the hill to Dad's grave, the dog jumped up and down, wagged his tail, and licked her all over. She couldn't help but laugh! That dog was so loving, and so excited to see her."

And yet there was something surreal about the scene. Given that the day was bitterly cold, why would a dog stay out in the open on top of a hill? There were fir trees nearby, where he could have gone to be sheltered from the wind. And instead of lying on his side, the dog had been covering the grave with his body, his head on the ground as if he were a sentinel guarding it.

"That's strange," Marilyn's mother murmured, looking intently at the dog.

"What, Mom?" Marilyn asked.

"That dog. He looks exactly like Rusty."

"Who's Rusty?"

"He was your father's dog. The first one we ever had on the farm. They could be twins."

Marilyn looked back at the dog. By now everyone wanted to pet him, but he wouldn't have it. He ducked away from the outstretched hands, instead dancing in circles around Marilyn, his eyes searching her face as if he was performing just for her, his tail fanned out in the wind. It was obvious to everyone there that he had chosen Marilyn to love.

The women left him a plate of food that night. "We went back in the morning," Mary said, "and sure enough, he was still protecting my dad's grave. We got out of the car and again, it was my sister that the dog chose. He lavished her with kisses, all over her face. He wagged his tail. He ran circles around her, excited as if she were a long-lost friend." He would have nothing to do with Mary, even though she had a large piece of meat in her hand for him.

The women left him another plate of food and some water. Marilyn went back three times that day to see him. Mary noticed that her sister's misery seemed to be lifting just a little.

That night the women phoned their neighbors, asking if anyone had a dog like the one at the cemetery. No one within a five-mile radius recognized his description. "I'm going to take him home," Marilyn told Mary. "It's so cold, and he obviously doesn't have a place to go."

"And he certainly loves you!" Mary added. The dog still had eyes only for Marilyn. There seemed to be a special bond between them, one that neither woman had ever experienced. If Marilyn took him home, it would be a perfect solution.

But the next day, the dog was gone. As quickly as he had come, he vanished.

Marilyn came back from the cemetery with the news. She had called and whistled and walked the entire area, but there was no sign of the dog. Could he have decided to go back to his earlier home? Both women went back to the snow-covered hill. As Marilyn had said, the dog was gone. *Come back*, Mary whispered to him. *Come back and give my sister some hope.* They had just started to recover from their father's death, and now the grieving would begin anew. "Where could he have gone?" Marilyn asked, bewildered. "And why?"

The answer came suddenly to Mary, the words a blessing. "Do you remember that passage from the Apostle's Creed?" she asked Marilyn. "The one that says, 'On the third day He rose again from the dead'?"

Marilyn met her eyes. "It's the third day since we saw the dog, isn't it? Do you suppose he came to guide Dad to heaven?"

Mary had no doubt. Her father had known how devastated his daughter was and had arranged for a special angel to come and ease her mourning. God took what had been a hard time for them and turned it into a miracle.

The dog never reappeared, but the Doubler family knows where he is. They look forward to seeing him—and their father—again.

SPECIAL SECTION

Children and Angels

Bolt Out of the Blue

Sharon Thompson

PLAYING ON MY FAMILY'S OLD metal swing set was one of my favorite things to do. I loved the feeling of soaring over the earth with the cool wind in my hair. One afternoon, my sister and I were so busy swinging we didn't notice the sky had darkened.

"Girls, come inside!" my mother yelled from the front porch. We jumped off the swing set and dashed toward safety.

Kay was faster.

I followed her underneath the fifteen-foot-long wire that connected our TV antenna to the house. The antenna sat on top of an old tree trunk. Just as I crossed under the wire, lightning struck the tree. Electricity ran through the wire above me and through the tree into the ground. There was a jolt, and then warm arms wrapped around me. Someone shielded me until the lightning passed.

"There was a man with you!" Kay said when we were all safe on the porch.

My mother looked me over to see if I was okay. She found two large handprints on either side of my head. They reached from my ears to the bottom of my neck, and lasted for several hours. But I had never felt any pain—only the gentle touch of a guardian angel who had swooped in to shelter me from the storm.

Short Trip, Big Save

Joan Sapp

IT WAS A SHORT DRIVE home from the day care center, so my daughter-in-law let my three-year-old grandson, Isaiah, ride in the front seat. The car went off the road and flipped over before coming to a rest on its wheels. My daughter-in-law looked for Isaiah. The seat beside her was empty. Isaiah was sitting in the backseat—completely unharmed. He crawled into his mother's lap to wait for help.

A few days later, I asked Isaiah what he remembered. "Jesus held me," Isaiah said. "He put me in the backseat. And I saw angels, Grammie. They were all around Mama!" After that we always used the car seat—no matter how short the trip.

A Mother's Guardian Dear

Henrietta Torres

BACK WHEN WE WERE A young couple, my husband, Bill, and I shared a bedroom with our seven-month-old baby, Steve, who slept in a crib near our full-sized bed.

One night, as my family lay sleeping, I sensed someone in the room with us. I opened my eyes and saw an angel standing by Steve's crib. He was tall, and his large wings filled half the room. His wings and robe glowed with a soft bluish light. He gazed at my sleeping son.

When I blinked, the angel was gone. Gone from my sight, perhaps, but ever near my child.

Later, cleaning around Steve's crib, I saw a terrible sight—a black widow spider and her nest. I knew then why the blue angel had come.

Joseph

Helen K. Basile

I WAS A YOUNG NURSE, just four years out of St. Clare's Hospital School of Nursing in New York City. Our training by the beautiful Franciscan nuns prepared us well, not only to serve the physical needs of our patients but also to be open to seeing the face of Jesus in them.

My five-year-old cousin Joseph was in the hospital and scheduled to have his tonsils out. While there, the doctors discovered a lump in the side of his neck. This little guy, so young and so pure, was diagnosed with sarcoma, and at that time there was no hope for remission or a cure. Medicine has come a long way in the last forty years, but in those days, a diagnosis like Joseph's was a death sentence.

During the next few months, every effort was made to keep him comfortable and unafraid and to support his young parents, who were devastated. Two months after the initial diagnosis, Joseph was back in the hospital, a very sick little boy, and his time with us was growing short. There were no hospices at that time, and it was the norm to remain in the hospital to die.

It was Easter time, and I had promised to stay with him on Holy Saturday night, from four to midnight. "Can you see the angels and the beautiful gold lights shining from them?" Joseph asked. "The music is beautiful too. Can you hear them singing?"

I remember telling him that I could because he would get upset when I did not answer him right away or when I said I could not see them too. Although this was a new experience for me, I did not doubt him or his experience for a moment. At the time, I wondered why I did not doubt what he was telling me.

He told me his dad was going to buy a new blue suit for him, and that he was going to wear it when he went to see Jesus. His dad called to check on him at about 10:00 PM, and I told him Joseph was resting well and seemed peaceful. I shared with him all the things Joseph had told me about the angels and the beautiful music. His dad took it all in quietly, not saying a word but somehow knowing that Joseph was going to leave this earth soon. I finished my four-to-twelve shift and headed home, telling Joseph I would see him again the next day.

His parents had arranged for a private-duty nurse from twelve to eight in the morning—in those days parents were not encouraged to stay overnight with a family member. Nursing staff at that time was not as open to discussing the impending death of a child as they are today. If hospice and end-of-life care was as understood and prevalent then as it is now, the nurses would have been talking to Joseph and his family about the immediacy of his going to heaven, and they in turn would have been better prepared. That was simply not done at the time, which made it more difficult for everyone. Death was shrouded in mystery.

I heard the phone ring in the hallway at home at around 7:00 AM, and my mother crying. "Yes," she said. "I will go and tell her now." She came into my room and told me that the angels had come for Joseph at about six o'clock and had taken him into heaven with them. His dad was going to the store when they opened to buy a blue suit for Joseph, just as he had told me.

Although this experience happened forty-seven years ago, it is as fresh in my mind as if it happened yesterday.

When Jesus said to let the little children come to Him for the kingdom of heaven belonged to them, I think this is what He was speaking about. The simplicity and purity of their lives is what Jesus was telling us to follow in order to be like Him. The confidence and trust Joseph reflected as he was dying is what Jesus wants us to experience throughout our lives. In that way, we will be at peace when it is our time to go home to Him.

Be open, always, to the youngest and the oldest around you. Jesus will make Himself known to you in some of the most tender and delicate ways you can ever imagine. The kingdom of God is all around us. You just have to reach out and touch it to follow in His footsteps.

Breathe Easy, Baby Sister

Elizabeth Veldboom

EVEN THOUGH I WAS ONLY five, I could see how frazzled my mother was. My baby sister, Rachel, had respiratory syncytial virus, which made it very difficult for her to breathe. My parents had to watch her every second.

One night I awoke after midnight to an extraordinary sight: Two gigantic angels with huge wings stood guard over Rachel's crib. Their presence made me feel safe because I knew my baby sister was safe. When Mom cracked open the door to check on us I wanted her to feel safe too. "Angels are here!" I said.

"Where?" she whispered.

I pointed over at Rachel's crib. The next morning, Mom said she got the best rest she'd had in weeks that night. Rachel is now a healthy, happy fourteen-year-old. It's hard to imagine her struggling for breath. But there are those of us who know better: me, my mom, and Rachel's two angels.

Feathers of Protection

Steven Eaton

I RACED FROM MY OFFICE to the hospital. Our thirteen-year-old son, Jacob, was involved in an auto accident with a family friend. "It's okay, Dad," Jacob said when I got to him. His clothes were blood-stained, but luckily he only had some cuts and scrapes on his arms and legs. I hugged him more tightly than ever before. While the doctors conferred, Jacob confided in me: "Something amazing happened when the car crashed, Dad. I felt something feathery cover me. Something like an angel's wing."

When I saw pictures of the wrecked car I had no doubts about the feeling Jacob described. There was an angel in the car. My son would not have survived without heavenly protection. You always hope as a parent that angels are watching out for your kids. Now I know for sure.

Picture This

Cee Cee Clark

WE'D JUST LEFT A FAMILY reunion with our grandchildren, four-year-old Chad and eleven-year-old Bailey. As my husband and I drove off, Bailey asked, "Granny, where is Uncle Dick's grave?" Uncle Dick died long before the grandkids were born, but we always told them stories about his days playing college football. They felt like they knew him.

"Nearby," I said. "Why don't we go for a visit?"

We pulled into the cemetery and walked to Dick's grave. We read his headstone and said a prayer. As we were leaving, Chad turned around. "Wait! I want to see the angel again!" he said.

"What angel?" I asked.

"She was standing right there," he said. "She had big white wings! She was right here," Chad insisted.

I hugged Chad close. "I know you saw her," I said. "She was a special angel sent just for you."

At home, I sketched an angel. Chad said it looked exactly like her. "Would you like me to paint a picture of her for you?" Chad thought about it for a moment. "How about a shark instead?" It made me think angels for Chad are an everyday occurrence. And why shouldn't we think of them as such?

Caught

Jolene DuFour

SKIING AFTER DINNER, YEAH! MOM'S a ski instructor, and she taught my brother, Chris, and me. Our whole family would hit the slopes right after dinner to take advantage of the discounted evening rates. I couldn't wait. There was nothing I loved more than racing my big brother down the mountain.

Not that Chris wanted much to do with me these days. He was eleven and wanted to hang out with his friends without his eight-year-old kid sister tagging along. Like now. He was playing ball with his buddies. I sat on the porch and watched. *I'll catch up to him on the slopes tonight*, I thought, looking out at the sunset.

The sky was turning all these cool colors. It reminded me of the dream I'd woken up from that morning. In my dream I floated effortlessly in an indigo sky, puffy white clouds all around me. I felt tingly, warm, and above all, protected—as safe as I felt back when Chris used to walk me to school.

"Chris, Jolene, dinner!" my mother called. Chris waved to his friends and followed me inside. Mom, Dad, and our baby sister, April, were already at the table. Dad barely finished grace before Chris and I wolfed down our food and ran to get our skis and snow gear. I threw on my favorite pink snowsuit and matching gloves. Then my brother and I loaded the car with all of our equipment.

As soon as we got on the slopes I snapped into my bindings and took off after Chris. I caught up to him at the chairlift. We stood in line together. Finally, it was our turn. At exactly the same time we hopped on the chairs coming up behind us. At the top of the mountain, Chris challenged me to a race. He counted us off. Down we went. The powdery snow felt like silk under my skis. We zipped down the mountain, shifting our bodies with every turn. At the bottom I kicked up a velvety spray of snow. "*Yesss!*" I'd won! I didn't win many races, but when I did it was a huge victory. "You won't get lucky like that again, Sis," Chris said. We pushed off toward the chairlift again.

The sky on the mountain range deepened to cobalt blue. "Time to go home, kids," Mom said.

"Just one more run!" Chris and I begged. It felt like we had just gotten there.

"Okay, guys. But this is it," she said. I nodded and turned to follow Chris. He was already at the chairlift.

"He left me!" I cried. I didn't want to take my last run alone.

"Don't worry, honey," Mom said. "I'll ski with you." Mom handed April to Dad. Impatiently, I pulled her to the chairlift. We stood facing front, just like I'd done a hundred times before. I looked over my shoulder. The lift was coming up behind us faster than usual. Out of the corner of my eye I saw Mom hop on. *Whack!* The chair hit me in the back. *Wait!* The lift moved forward and up. I jumped for the chair. *It's too high!* Mom grabbed me under the arms. My snowsuit was slippery. She couldn't get a good grip. "Stop the lift!" the man in the chair behind us yelled. "A little girl is falling! Stop the lift!"

But it kept climbing. Mom frantically clutched me. I slid. She had me by the elbows. Then only by my gloved hands.

"Mom!" I screamed.

"Hold on, baby!" she yelled.

The chair soared above the trees. I could see snow blowing off the tops of the branches. People on the ground looked like little dots.

Inside my gloves I could feel my fingers slipping from my mother's grasp.

"Jolene!" Mom gasped.

Then, *whoosh*, I was falling. I looked up at the sapphire sky. But somehow I wasn't scared. I felt warm and protected. Just like in my dream the night before. My arms and legs moved in slow motion, like I was floating, like something was holding me up in the air.

A blazing white light flashed before me. I landed, skis flat on the ground, in a patch of hard-packed snow. The cold wind whipped across my face.

Where was Mom? The next thing I knew she was standing over me, tears in her eyes. "Oh, baby," she whispered.

The ski patrol came and put me in a brace and a basket. Then they whisked me down the mountain to the hospital.

They did all kinds of tests and X-rays in the emergency room. All they could find were a few bruises.

"You are a very lucky young lady," the doctor said. "You fell more than forty feet. If you had landed slightly forward or slightly back, you could have been killed." Mom hugged me tight. I turned my head and noticed my whole family standing there next to the hospital bed. I'd never seen my big brother look so upset.

"Jolene, I'm sorry I left you all alone on the mountain," Chris said. "I should have waited for you."

"It's okay, Chris," I said. "I wasn't alone. Someone was with me the whole time." Someone Who will protect me, waking, dreaming, falling...always.

Golden Angel

Louise Tucker Jones

WE HAD TO BEGIN HOME-SCHOOLING our son Jay because he had Down syndrome and a serious congenital heart condition that was worsening. Now, at seventeen and without classmates, Jay was isolated. I worried about his being lonely.

At night I knelt at his bedside and asked what he wanted to pray for. Sometimes it was hard to understand his speech, but with gestures and sign language, Jay got his request across. It might be for his brother at college or for his grandparents. But lately he grinned and said: "Angel."

What he really needs is a friend, I told God, a buddy to play with. Jay prized his collection of G.I. Joes, tanks and helicopters, and it broke my heart to see him playing with them alone. Sometimes, though, it almost seemed like the toys played back. Once, a grinding noise and white light came alive in the corner. Startled, I jumped onto his bed! He laughed and pointed to a copter. Its lights and propeller were activated by pressing a button. How had the crazy thing turned itself on?

Another time I found a remote-controlled army tank rolling across Jay's floor at 2:00 AM, its red light flashing in the dark while Jay slept peacefully. My husband explained it away as having "something to do with radio waves."

One particular night the room was quiet. "Angel," Jay prompted me again. Then he looked toward the door and grinned. It dawned on me that he had repeated this routine for weeks. "Jay, what are you grinning at?" He pointed.

I looked around. "What is it? What do you see?" My son grew frustrated. "An angel?" I guessed.

"Yeah!"

"Where?" I asked. Jay motioned toward the door. He animatedly explained that an angel had been standing there every night, and sometimes spoke to him. He had tried to tell me for weeks. I asked him to describe the angel. With his thumb and pinkie Jay signed: "Yellow."

"You mean the angel's clothes are yellow?"

"Yeah."

What about his face, his hair? Again he signed "Yellow." Jay couldn't use words like golden or shining, so his description made sense: My son had a golden angel for a companion. And a playful one, at that.

I often stop at the doorway and ask this friend to stay close to my son while he sleeps. And now when I hear the toys whirring in the night, I know Jay's golden angel is on duty.

When Grandpa Said Good-bye

James L. Garlow & Keith Wall

JENNIFER TURNED IN THE CUSHIONED chair and tried to find a more comfortable position. As hospital waiting rooms went, this one wasn't bad—furnished more like a living room than the cold, sterile rooms in some medical facilities. But still, she and her family had spent many long hours here, sitting, praying, holding vigil, and waiting for the heartbreaking news that Ron was really gone.

Ron Wallace was Jennifer's stepfather, and at fifty-three he seemed a young candidate for myelodysplastic syndrome, the rare bone marrow disorder that would soon claim his life. Four months earlier, he had begun the tedious and lengthy process of receiving a bone marrow transplant in the hope of staving off the disease. But when a freak infection spread to his brain, he was transferred from the cancer ward to ICU. His family was notified: It wouldn't be much longer now.

It was night, and Jennifer wished she could find a way to fall asleep in the waiting room. She was so tired. She closed her eyes. She actually began to drift into a restless sleep. Suddenly she was awakened by flickering lights. She opened her eyes. The bright overhead lights were glowing solidly, without a flicker in sight. She thought to herself, *Maybe I'm seeing angels.*

She tried to fall asleep several more times, but every time she got close to crossing over into slumber, she was aroused by flickering lights before her eyes. Finally she sat up and looked at her sister, Laura, who was also wide-awake.

"You can't sleep either, huh?" Jennifer asked.

Laura said, "Every time I fall asleep I see angels flying around the room and lights flashing."

Jennifer stared at her sister a full minute before responding. "Really?" That's strange. And you know what's even stranger? I keep seeing the same thing."

Ron had come into their lives nineteen years earlier when he married their mother. He had been a good stepfather to Carol's four daughters. He had been an even more amazing grandfather to his fifteen grandchildren. He was the kind of grandpa who was forever taking one of the kids fishing, to the park, or out for ice cream.

The night passed slowly. Around daybreak, a doctor approached the family and said it was just a matter of time. They took Ron off the ventilator and began allowing family members into his room to say their good-byes.

Jennifer and her sisters discussed whether or not to let their children in the room to say good-bye to their grandfather. Jennifer's eight-year-old son, Chris, and Laura's four-year-old daughter, Kira, wanted desperately to see Grandpa Ron one more time before he died. But the skin on Ron's face was turning black as the tissue began to die—something that can happen in the last hours of life—plus he was unconscious, so he couldn't have said anything to the children.

In the end, the sisters decided that the disease had so ravaged Ron's body that his grandchildren would be better off not seeing him in his final hours. And so the children stayed with relatives in the waiting room. They were nearby—the waiting room happened to be adjacent to Ron's room in ICU—and that would have to do.

In the final hours of her stepdad's life, Jennifer thought about the flickering lights she and Laura had seen each time they'd started to doze. She looked into the space above the bed where her stepfather lay dying. The air seemed empty, but was it really? Were angels there? Angels that could be glimpsed in the twilight between consciousness and sleep? Angels that had congregated in the thin space between life and death?

Ron died around four o'clock that afternoon. The girls cried and tried to comfort their mother, Carol. About ten minutes later, Jennifer headed toward the waiting room to let Ron's grandkids know that he was gone. As she walked into the room, Chris jumped up and ran to his mother.

"Mom, Grandpa just died," he blurted.

Jennifer nodded. "He did. How did you know?"

"A few minutes ago I was getting tired so I sat down and started falling asleep, and just as I did, Grandpa came to me in a dream and told me he loved me and would miss me, but it was time for him to go to heaven. And, Mom, there were angels all around Grandpa, and they were singing this really amazing song. Then Grandpa waved to me, and I woke up."

Jennifer's husband, Mike, joined them as Chris finished telling his mom about his dream. No one else knew about Chris's experience. So when another grandchild had the same dream that night, the family took note.

It was four-year-old Kira this time. She awoke on the morning after Ron's death singing a song. When her mother asked what she was singing, Kira said simply, "Grandpa was in my dream. He told me he loved me, but he was going to live in heaven and he would see me again one day. And there were angels everywhere, and they were singing this song." Kira began to sing again and, indeed, sang that song for several weeks.

Kira and Chris had begged to be in the room with their grandpa when he died. Instead, they'd been in the waiting room. Is that why Ron appeared to them? To comfort them in their grief and disappointment at being so close yet not being allowed into the ICU? Or perhaps their senses had been sharpened as they waited in the same room where Jennifer and Laura had already sensed the presence of angels.

A third child had taken Ron's death particularly hard. Five-year-old Ashlee lived with her mother in a house they had shared with Grandpa Ron. She had loved her grandpa so much she had shaved her head during his illness out of solidarity and support.

One night, about a week after Ron had died, Ashlee got out of bed to go to the bathroom, which was next to the room that had belonged to her grandfather when he was alive. Still aching at his absence, Ashlee walked slowly down the hallway and past his room. The hallway was dimly lit, the only light coming from a night-light in the bathroom. So Ashlee walked gingerly with her head down, watching her feet to avoid stumbling. Suddenly she walked into someone and fell backward, landing in a sitting position on the floor. Looking up, she saw her grandpa.

"Ashlee, what are you doing up?"

"Grandpa! What are you doing here? They said you died!"

Her grandpa squatted down so he could look her in the eyes. "I just came to check on you and tell you that I love you." He smiled and nodded toward Ashlee's room. "Now get on back to bed." And with that, he was gone.

One thing the experience taught Jennifer Mizicko and the rest of her family members: Death is never final, and good-bye is not forever. "All of the amazing events surrounding my stepdad's death showed us that the dividing line between life on earth and life beyond hardly exists," she said. "We are spiritual creatures living in physical bodies. One day, each of us will shed our bodies, but our spirits will go right on living."

Angel by Her Side

Carol Wolfenberger

WE ALL STRUGGLED WHEN MY husband died, but my youngest daughter, Jill, simply couldn't bring herself to talk about it. My prayers were for God to bring her comfort.

One evening after visiting with her children, she got in the car to leave and began crying.

"What's wrong, Mom?" five-year-old Harrison asked.

"I miss Paw-Paw," Jill explained.

"Don't cry," Harrison said. "Paw-Paw is sitting right beside you."

Jill glanced at the empty passenger seat. Reagan, age seven, smiled big.

"Look! He's right there," Harrison pointed.

I think an angel sat beside Jill. A comforting angel who would be there to listen when she was ready.

Acknowledgments

THIS CONSTITUTES A CONTINUATION OF the copyright page. Every attempt has been made to credit the sources of copyrighted material used in this book. If any such acknowledgment has been inadvertently omitted or miscredited, receipt of such information would be appreciated.

"An Angel in Every Lap," "A Motorcycle Miracle," "Angels in Blue Jeans" and "Love in the Lava" are reprinted by permission from the author. Copyright © 2011 by Joan Wester Anderson.

"Angel in the Cemetery" and "To Sir, With Love" excerpt from Angelic Tails: True Stories of Heavenly Canine Companions by Joan Wester Anderson (Loyola Press, 2011). Reprinted with permission from Loyola Press. To order copies call 1-800-621-1008 or go to www.loyolapress.com.

"An Angel Picked Me Up and We Flew," "Angels All Around," "Mountaintop Miracle" and "When Grandpa Said Good-bye" from Encountering Heaven and the Aft erlife by James L. Garlow and Kevin Wall. Used by permission of Bethany House Publishers, a division of Baker Publishing Group. Copyright © 2010 by James L. Garlow and Keith Wall.

"Angel's Miracle" is reprinted by permission from the author. Copyright © 2012 Janice E. Nash.

"Angels from Interpol" is reprinted from the book Th e Promise of Hope, copyright © 2011 by Edward Grinnan and published by Guideposts Books. Used by permission from the author.

"Bagpipes in Heaven" from Miracles Are for Real by James L. Garlow and Kevin Wall. Used by permission of Bethany House Publishers, a division of Baker Publishing Group. Copyright © 2011 by James L. Garlow and Keith Wall.

"Th e Dolphins Saved My Life" from the book Angel Animals. Copyright © 1999, 2007 by Allen and Linda Anderson. Reprinted with permission of New World Library, Novato, CA.

"A Gift of Love" is reprinted by permission from the author. Copyright © 2011 by Sophy Burnham.

"Joseph" and "Mr. Winters" from More Glimpse of Heaven by Trudy Harris, RN. Used by permission of Revell, a division of Baker Publishing Group. Copyright © 2010 by Trudy Harris.

"The Lady with Red Hair" is reprinted by permission from the author. Copyright © 2012 by Morna Gilbert.

"Midnight Visit" from the book Angel Dogs. Copyright © 2005 by Allen and Linda Anderson. Reprinted with permission of New World Library, Novato, CA.

"Pull In" is reprinted by permission from the author. Copyright © 2012 by Jackie Osinski.

"A Secret for Five," "Th e Tall Visitor" and "Help Wanted: Divine Domestic" from Angels, Miracles and Heavenly Encounters by James Stuart Bell. Used by permission of Bethany House Publishers, a division of Baker Publishing Group. Copyright © 2012 Whitestone Communications, Inc.

Acknowledgments

"Special Order" by Lorraine Newkirk as told to Connie Lounsbury is reprinted by permission from the author. Copyright © 2012 by Connie Lounsbury.

"Touched by an Angel" is reprinted by permission from the author. Copyright © 2012 by Jennifer Clark Vihel.

To Our Readers

CONARI PRESS, AN IMPRINT OF Red Wheel/Weiser, publishes books on topics ranging from spirituality, personal growth, and relationships to women's issues, parenting, and social issues. Our mission is to publish quality books that will make a difference in people's lives—how we feel about ourselves and how we relate to one another. We value integrity, compassion, and receptivity, both in the books we publish and in the way we do business.

Our readers are our most important resource, and we appreciate your input, suggestions, and ideas about what you would like to see published.

Visit our website at *www.redwheelweiser.com* to learn about our upcoming books and free downloads, and be sure to go to *www.redwheelweiser.com/newsletter/* to sign up for newsletters and exclusive offers.

You can also contact us at *info@rwwbooks.com*.

Conari Press
an imprint of Red Wheel/Weiser, LLC
665 Third Street, Suite 400
San Francisco, CA 94107